The Royal Cracow

EUROPEAN CITIES OF CULTURE

AVIGNON

BERGEN

BOLOGNA

BRUXELLES

KRAKÓW

HELSINKI

PRAHA

REYKJAVÍK

SANTIAGO DE COMPOSTELA

The Royal Cracow
Adam Bujak

Introduction by
prof. Jan K. Ostrowski

„Biały Kruk" Publishing House

Ukochanemu Ojcu Świętemu —
Janowi Pawłowi II

W przededniu Trzeciego Tysiąclecia Naszej Wiary
pracę tę poświęcam

Adam Bujak

I dedicate this work to the beloved Pope, John Paul II, on the eve of the Third Millennium of Our Faith.

Adam Bujak

Publisher
Leszek Sosnowski

Graphic design
Władysław Pluta
Ewa Tarnawska

Editor
Jolanta Sosnowska

Desktop Publishing
Wojciech Bartkowski

German translation
Jolanta Sosnowska
Language consultant
Otto Riegler

English translation
Krystyna Haupt
Eunika Bogucka

Captions
Anna Szczucka

Proof-reading
Ewa Kłeczek

Manager
Sepp Karer

Colour scanning
„Skonto" Zbigniew Sułkowski

Printed by
Helios Exprint, Czech Republic

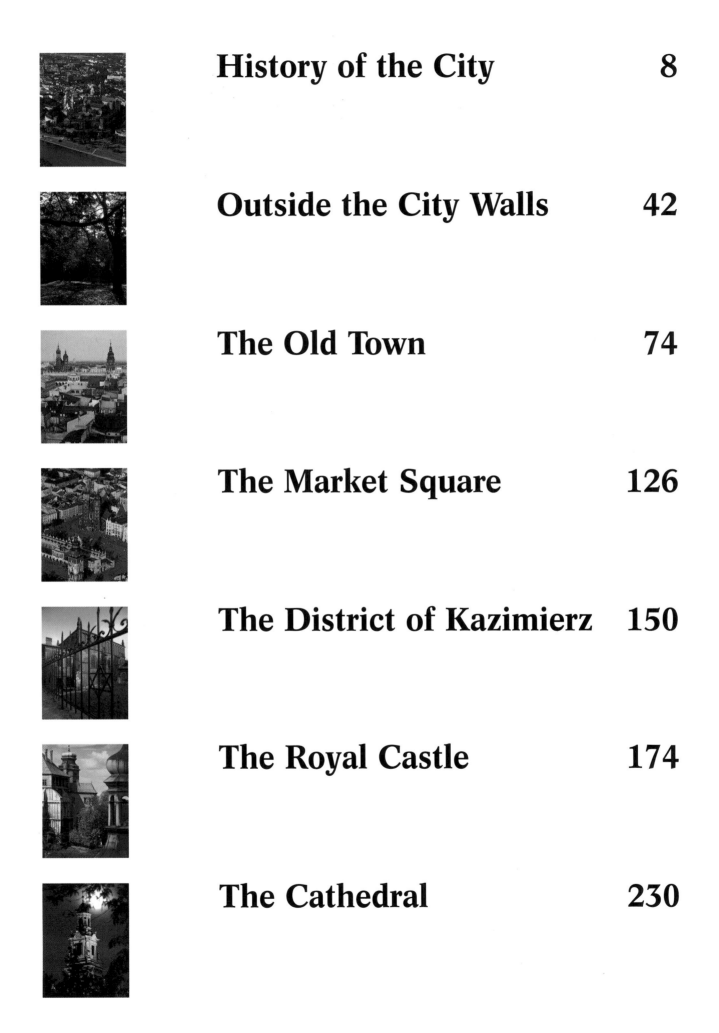

History of the City

Towns are not born by chance. It is usually a long and difficult process to gather a certain number of people in a given location, to make them stay there permanently and to transform them into a uniform social structure. The beginning is mostly due to the will of an individual having power or large financial means, the needs of a state or specific economic circumstance. It is often easier to build a town than to make it survive through the changing fates.

So many once flourishing centres have been devoured by a jungle or by a desert, and so many are known to us only thanks to the studies of historians or archaeologists.

Dead towns are often treasured as a fossil, a genuine document of the distant past, giving evidence of the scale of evolution undergone by humanity as well as of the amazing similarity between us and our distant ancestors. Much more fascinating however are towns proud of their hundreds or sometimes even thousands years old tradition, presenting a wide spectrum of various epochs and cultures and at the same time enjoying a full, dynamic and modern life.

Towns differ considerably. This category covers both big capitals and little towns which squat near ancient routes, separated from each other by the distance covered in one day by a mediaeval traveller. The main and nearly only function of these towns was to provide rest and safety to such a traveller. There are obviously few capitals and only several European centres in larger countries that have maintained leading political, cultural and economic positions throughout the ages. The real metropolises of the continent are Rome and Paris. London and Madrid were usually the periphery of European matters, but they ruled over overseas realms. The star of Vienna lost its brightness with the fall of the Hapsburg dynasty. The old St. Petersburg was said to be the only real capital apart from Paris, though this cannot be said about Moscow, with its expansionism, chaos and ubiquitous ugliness even despite its role as the centre of a still awe inspiring power. The uniting Europe, more obviously continues to promote the still provincial Brussels to the rank of its capital. And what more is there? In fact, not much. The next category of towns which count on the map of the continent are usually medium size towns (not many realise that Florence, Geneva and Zurich, each have less than half a million inhabitants), which have grown due to their cultural or economic role. Cracow can be included in this category as the old capital of the then extensive territory of Poland, which along with Prague, Budapest, Vienna and Nuremberg represents one of the historic capitals of Central Europe.

Throughout over a thousand years of its documented existence,

Cracow was a seat of princes and kings; an abandoned and slowly dying out capital of a big country; a provincial town of the Austrian Empire, but at the same time functioned as a "town - symbol" for the Polish nation, reconstructing its identity under the foreign rule. At the turn of 19th and 20th centuries it was a flourishing cultural centre, later a capital of Nazi occupied Province with the headquarters of the notorious Governor Hans Frank. Finally, for the communist rulers it was a symbol of Polish opposition which had to be punished and suppressed by building the industrial district of Nowa Huta next to the old city. What is the Cracow of today? A museum city or a cluster of pseudomodern blocks of flats? A centre of science and culture or perhaps mostly of industry, the presence of which one cannot forget even for a minute? Or perhaps Cracow is simply a community which wants life in dignity, looking back to its past but thinking mostly of the coming 21st century? The answers to these questions depend on the individual perspective. One thing is certain - both the old and new Cracow has a specific image of its own. Though surrounded with ugly blocks of flats, impoverished and treated as a second class town for dozens of years, it has not lost its unique individuality. What is more, it has maintained and developed it during the most difficult time. Tadeusz Kantor, Sławomir Mrożek and Krzysztof Penderecki, the "Tygodnik Powszechny" weekly and the "Piwnica pod Baranami" cabaret already belong to the historic influences of the town. Similarly as Veit Stoss, Jan Matejko and Stanisław Wyspiański, with the "Czas" newspaper and the "Zielony Balonik" cabaret of the old times. One of the main objectives of this book is to show this unique quality of Cracow.

The thousand-year history of Cracow must have been based on certain stable grounds. One of them was a favourable location at the crossing of the major trading routes near a ford on the Vistula River which served as the most important traffic artery of the country. The second one was Wawel Castle, the best possible seat of the centre of power, controlling a vast territory. Apart from that, the natural conditions for starting a town were not particularly convenient. Its later site consisted mostly of vast shallows full of marshes and ponds, densely criss-crossed by the Vistula and the Rudawa tributaries. For obvious reasons, the original settlements concentrated on the higher and dry points, thus apart from the Wawel Hill, one of the oldest settlements was built in the Salwator area. The ridge leading from Wawel to the north, along Grodzka, Floriańska and Sławkowska Streets, plotted the direction of the main traffic routes and one axis of the future town. Urban development required progressive regulation of the water system and draining of new areas of land.

The oldest traces of human settlements in Cracow date back to the distant Palaeolithic times. There are also remains coming from Neolithic, bronze and iron cultures. The Celts, who came around 300 B.C., brought with them remarkable progress towards greater civilisation. In the early years after Christ, the borders of the Roman Empire approached the southern Lesser Poland. Metal works and pottery centres began to appear in the area but primitive farming and forestry still prevailed. This period of development was interrupted by the great migrations around the half of the first millennium. The next, more remarkable, archaeological findings as well as the first, not very accurate mentions relating to the surroundings of Cracow, which was by then one of the main strongholds of the tribal Wiślanie state, come only from the 9th century. The state confronted the neighbouring power, Great Moravia, and most probably had to surrender, and its ruler whose name is not known was forced to accept Christianity. The town then included, apart from the Wawel Hill, the so-called Okół located in the north, at the foot of hill which reached Senacka Street. The population of the stronghold and the settlement is estimated to have been around 1400 people. No architectural remains, in the common meaning of this word, have survived from the tribal period. We only know the mysterious earth mounds named after Wanda and Krakus and the remnants of fortifications and wooden structures still excavated by archaeologists.

By the mid 10th century the Wiślanie state with Cracow, came to be ruled by Bohemia. Around 965, an Arab merchant of Jewish origin, Ibrahim ibn Yaqub, in the description of his travels through the Slav countries mentions a town of "Krakwa" as belonging to the lands of the Bohemian King, Boleslaus. In this way Cracow entered written history and soon afterwards, together with the whole Lesser Poland was incorporated into the State of the Piasts. The integration was strengthened by establishing, in the year 1000, the Cracow episcopacy subordinated to the bishops of Gniezno. Christian traditions were obviously much older here; we even know the names of the local half-legendary bishops - Prochor and Prokulf. The oldest known church in Cracow is the Wawel Rotunda dedicated to St. Felix and St. Adauctus. At the beginning of the eleventh century two more, apart from the first Wawel Cathedral, churches were built - St. Adalbert's in the present Market Square and St. Salvator's in the Zwierzyniec area. Both were probably erected to replace the earlier pagan temples.

As it seems the civil war, known as the pagan reaction, and the Bohemian invasion, which caused deep crisis of the early Piast monarchy in the 1030's, seemed to spare Cracow. The town became the main support centre for Prince Casimir

the Restorer (Odnowiciel) in his attempt to rebuild the country. Starting from the turn of the 30's and 40's, Cracow became the seat of Polish rulers and soon established its function as the capital of the country. This function had to continue until 1609, and in the legal sense until the partitions, that took place towards the end of the eighteenth century.

In his great task of reconstructing a monarchy, Casimir the Restorer made use of the family links his mother had with Rhineland and Westerwald. From there came people, mostly clergymen, who served as the ruler's chief advisors. It is probable that the first Poles, who later filled high church and state offices were educated there as well. These contacts with the West determined for centuries the nature of the Romanesque art, which at that time found its way to Poland. The reconstruction undertaken by Casimir the Restorer was successful enough to allow his son Boleslaus the Bold (Śmiały) to launch expansionist policy against Ruthenia and Hungary and to become a crowned king of Poland in 1076. The following years brought about a great political and moral drama. As result of a conflict between the Cracow Bishop Stanislaus of Szczepanów and Boleslaus, the former lost his life and the latter had to leave the country forever. The details of the conflict, interpreted in many different ways by historians, will probably remain a mystery due to insufficient source materials. The only certainty is that the Bishop, pronounced a martyr and canonised in 1254, became a patron saint of Poland. His worship, for ages to follow, served as a valuable ideological weapon in the struggle for the unity and freedom of the country.

During the reigns of Ladislaus Herman and Boleslaus the Wry-mouthed (Krzywousty), the point of gravity of the state moved towards the north and the west. Dividing the country among his sons in 1138, Boleslaus made Cracow the official capital and its ruler had to enjoy sovereignty over the other Dukes. We know much more about Cracow of the end of the eleventh and the twelfth century. This period left us with much richer sources than before and with monumental sacral buildings. The main settlement of that time was located in the Okół, in the neighbourhood of the St. Andrew's Church. It was erected thanks to the funds of Sieciech the Palatine between 1079 - 1098 and further developed probably at the turn of the 12th and 13th centuries. The church has still preserved its walls made of small limestone blocks, characteristic of the Cracow Romanesque style, and a massive western part crowned with two towers.

Since around 1090, a second Romanesque cathedral was under construction at the Wawel Hill. It became consecrated in 1142. What remains of this structure are the Silver Bells Tower and the Crypt of St. Leonard. This wonderfully preserved

Romanesque interior serves today as a necropolis of national Heroes. It is worth remembering however that in 1118 Cracow Bishop, Maurus, was buried here and that the historian and poet known as Gallus Anonimus dedicated his first Polish Chronicle to him. A cathedral school with a well stocked library must have existed then and its preserved inventories from the years 1101 and 1110 prove that at the beginning of the twelfth century there were scholars in Cracow who had good command of Latin and were well acquainted with the works of classical writers.

The period of Poland's division into principalities, amounting to almost 200 years, saw a continuous chain of conflicts and power struggles among the Piast dynasty members who sought to dominate the Cracow Duchy. Despite the succession rules established by the will of Boleslaus the Wry-mouthed it was strength that decided upon the control of Wawel Castle. Several dukes repeatedly won and lost the Cracow throne. Such circumstances increased the importance of Lesser Poland's noblemen who frequently decided upon the success or failure of the respective pretenders to the sovereign position.
The status gained by the Cracow officials secured them the highest state offices for a long period of time, until the loss of independence in the 18th century. Despite the prolonged political chaos, nearly every generation produced a ruler who attempted restoration of the country's unity. It was Ladislaus the Short (Łokietek) who finally conquered Cracow in 1306 and was there crowned a king of Poland, thus bringing back the tradition started by his 11th century ancestors.
The troubled times of the 12th and 13th centuries did not hinder the development of the town. The population kept growing and reached between 2 to 5 thousand by the middle of the 13th century. The number of craftsmen increased and trade was becoming more and more important. In the 1320's, Cracow already had administrators called "sołtysi" and a 1244 source reports that the town was governed by the Magdeburg Laws.
The Tartar invasion in 1241 only partially slowed the intensive development process. The seat of the municipal authority was at that time located south of the present Market Square in the area of Okół or the Dominican Church. The layout of the town is clear thanks to the location of churches of Romanesque origins of which there are twenty in Cracow. These sacral buildings, apart from their strictly religious functions, played an important role in the community life. They served as assembly halls and courtrooms and even as defence points like St. Andrew's Church which resisted the attack of the Tartars in 1241.
Besides being the capital of the sovereign principality, Cracow was also the main religious and cultural centre of Poland.

The growing cult of St. Stanislaus well served the idea of the country's unity. At least two outstanding personalities occupied the Cracow bishop's throne at that time - Wincenty Kadłubek, the author of "The Polish Chronicle" and Iwo Odrowąż, a brother of St. Hyacinth. New quality was introduced to the religious and social life of Cracow by the two mendicant orders - the Dominicans and the Franciscans who settled there at the turn of the 12th and 13th centuries. Contrary to the St. Benedict's monks, who chose life in seclusion, the new orders, drew on the spirit of new trends in the Church and were mainly involved in preaching Gospel and charity activities in urban communities. Owing to them Cracow gained the new spiritual and intellectual ideas and also the first marked wave of Italian artistic influence. Brick as the main construction material for temples, and formal solutions specific for Italy determined the earliest phase of the Cracow Gothic style represented by the oldest parts of the Dominican and Franciscan churches.

The formal beginning of Cracow as an organised urban community was the Charter granted in 1257 on the grounds of the Magdeburg Laws by Prince Boleslaus the Chaste (Wstydliwy), his mother Grzymisława and his wife the Blessed Cunegund (Kinga). The Charter specified the legal, economic, social and architectural framework of the newly started urban entity. The municipality was headed by a "wójt" (the chief administrator) who held a hereditary office and who was vassal to the prince. This structure changed over time and full powers were gained by the Town Council. The founding document contained significant economical privileges for the townspeople and helped to attract new inhabitants, primarily coming from Silesia and speaking German as their first language.
This determined the ethnic nature of the town for around two hundred and fifty years after.
The charter was accompanied by working out an ambitious plan intended to provide a proper framework for the expected development of the municipality. The then established layout has survived to the present day and still shapes the very centre of the city. The system is ancient and goes back to the tradition of a Roman military camp. Centrally placed is a large market square with the most important public buildings, functioning as the main trading centre. Each side of the square measures around 200 meters, which makes it one of the biggest historical squares in Europe. Its original structure was different.
There was very little empty space and blocks of buildings circled by a street occupied the centre. Its German name "Ring" gave origin to the Polish term for the main town square. From each side of the square run three streets which, together with the cross streets, form a regular chessboard pattern.

This symmetry is broken only in the south-east corner made by the funnel shaped end of Grodzka Street. It is a remnant of some older arrangement. This is where the route from Wawel Castle branched into roads leading to the north and to the west which now correspond to Floriańska and Sławkowska Streets. The crossroads were guarded by the ancient Church of St. Adalbert. The other, still visible irregularities of the town plan result from the earlier existing buildings and from the specific structure of a 13th century town. These, for example, are the environs of Our Lady's Church and of the so-called "Gródek" the old seat of the Cracow "wójt" as well as the location of St. John's Church forcing the sharp turn of Św. Tomasza Street.

Within the blocks marked by the network of streets there were building lots of strictly determined sizes, reaching towards the Main Market Square with their narrow sides and going deep into the block. This resulted in a typical burgher's house with a narrow façade and complex inner development to match the shape of a plot.

Even today, after over seven hundred years, the projections of majority of houses in the centre of Cracow result from the ownership relations established by the Great Charter. Even the baroque and 19th century broad façaded houses generally have their dimensions determined by the module of a mediaeval building lot.

Fortifications were an indispensable element of a mediaeval town. In 1268, Duke Leszek the Dark (Czarny) authorised the construction of defence walls around Cracow. Originally they had no connection with Wawel Castle which stressed the town's autonomy. This privilege was withdrawn by Ladislaus the Short (Łokietek) in 1312 after the rebellion of the German speaking inhabitants. He located a new town on the Okół and surrounded the formerly separate parts of the town with one wall. The mediaeval fortifications can be easily traced on the basis of their preserved western fragments including the Floriańska Gate, the neighbouring towers and the 15th century Barbican.

The urban structure of Cracow, established in 1257, was filled with Gothic architecture. There are few remnants from the early phase of the 13th century. Among others, such include the eastern section of the Franciscan Church, the Cistercian Monastery in Mogiła and the Floriańska Gate with some sections of the adjoining walls.

The monumental buildings of that time were mostly made from brick, using the characteristic regular pattern. The fortifications were made of stone and the majority of private houses were built of timber.

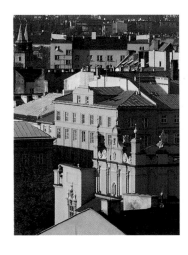

The coronation of King Ladislaus the Short in 1320 finally closed the long period of division and once again made Cracow the capital of a large kingdom. The extensive scale of the great foundation proved to be very useful in this situation, nevertheless the needs of the rapidly growing capital city led to establishment of satellite towns: - Kazimierz in 1335 and Kleparz in 1366. At that time Cracow was gradually acquiring the attributes of a big European city: the well developed system of craft guilds, trade privileges, the justice system based on German law, and finally the University founded in 1364 by King Casimir the Great. The population of Cracow at that time is estimated at 7 to 8 thousand. The townspeople were mostly craftsmen pursuing their trade in their own homes in the centre or building first industrial facilities, like mills, sawmills and tanneries in the outskirts of the town. The ethnic profile of mediaeval Cracow was diverse. Beside the Germans, prevailing among merchants and craftsmen, and Poles there were also Italians and a growing number of Jews. The Jews settled first in the area of the present Św. Anny Street and for that reason it was called "Żydowska" (Jewish) and later, in the eastern part of Kazimierz.

The fourteenth century witnessed the construction of a large number of public and private buildings many of which have been preserved to this day. The Town Hall with its tall tower and the Cloth Hall (Sukiennice), one of the symbols of Cracow, were built in the Market Square. The present Cloth Hall which at the first glance seems to be a Renaissance building (despite the 19th century additions) encases the 14th century structure, built by master Martin Linditolde. The city fortifications were constantly expanded as well as Wawel Castle which became the residence of a monarch aspiring to European status.

The 14th century is the first of all the classic period of Gothic religious architecture in Cracow. The first example is the Cathedral, the third one in the same location, started in 1320 and consecrated in 1364. The pillar and buttress construction system applied in the Cathedral was later followed in all the city churches. In 1355 reconstruction of the main city church, Our Lady's, was begun and soon afterwards that of the Dominican Church. Two large temples were built in Kazimierz - the Corpus Christi Church (1385-1405) and the Augustinian St. Catherine's (1345-14/15th c.) These churches were spacious brick basilicas in which the use of stone was limited to construction and decorative elements. The principal static problem was solved in a specific way by introducing buttresses relieving the weight of the nave vaulting, linked to pillars between the naves and hidden in the interior. In this way the builders avoided the use of flying buttresses, difficult in construction and prone to damage in the severe Polish climate. We know the names of a few Polish builders of

the 14th century. Beside the already mentioned Martin Lindintolde, they were Nicholas Werner who supervised the erection of the main section of Our Lady's Church and the Czipser family who were active in Kazimierz.

In the fourteenth century Cracow, one could notice for the first time, sculpture that was no longer subordinated to architecture. The most important examples are the Cathedral tombs of King Ladislaus the Short and King Casimir the Great. Preserved until today there are also some examples of wooden sculpture of that time which was to flourish in the next century.

There are not many fourteenth century paintings preserved. The most valuable specimens of this art are a set of approximately 120 stained glass panels in the presbytery of Our Lady's Church. After the recently finished conservation works they have almost completely regained their original colours and brilliance.

The coming to the throne of Ladislaus Jagiello in 1386 and the Union with Lithuania meant another promotion for Cracow. The monarch residing at Wawel ruled over one of the largest states in Europe covering the area of nearly a million square kilometres. The city entered its golden era and flourished for about 250 years. The 15th century was the period of internal peace and stability except for occasional unrests resulting from power struggles between the patrician and the plebeians and anti-Jewish manifestations.

The population grew to around ten thousand. New public and manufacturing facilities escalated. In 1399 Cracow obtained its water supply pipeline. In 1477 the first printed word in Poland appeared in this city. Of growing importance was the University, reinstituted in 1400 by Jagiello with the funds bequeathed in his wife Queen Hedwig's will. Its new organisation included the Theological Faculty, so important in view of the great task of the Christianization of Lithuania. The main building of the University at that time was Collegium Maius, gradually erected throughout the 15th and at the beginning of the 16th century and comprising a multiwinged edifice with a beautiful Gothic courtyard. In the 19th century it housed the Jagiellonian Library and now it functions as the University Museum. Around Collegium Maius grew the university district composed of colleges and dormitories and the University Church of St. Anne's. The Cracow University functioned in a way that closely resembled similar universities throughout Europe. Lectures were given in Latin, which allowed young people from different countries to enrol as students. The basic discipline taught at the Faculty of Liberated Arts was mediaeval scholasticism, but of growing importance were the works of ancient writers. The Faculties of Theology and Canon Law actively contributed to the great

European discussions concerning the structure of power in the Church and the Marian Dogmas. The greatest fame however, was gained by mathematics and the related disciplines of astronomy and... astrology. Nicolaus Copernicus was for some time a student of the Cracow University.

Considering the flourishing University life it is a paradox of some kind that the greatest Polish 16th century scholar was active outside its walls. Jan Długosz was a cathedral canon, a secretary to Cardinal Oleśnicki, a tutor of King Casimir Jagiellon's sons, and finally the Archbishop of Lvov. His life work is a monumental "History of Poland"; the basic source of all present studies on the mediaeval Poland. He also wrote a book of benefices of the diocese of Cracow - an invaluable source for research work on religious architecture, and even an illustrated catalogue of banners of the Teutonic Knights seized in the battle of Grunwald. The Latin used by Długosz is largely free from mediaeval deformities and shows the influence of Humanism. Towards the end of the 15th century the Humanism in Cracow acquired fully modern features thanks to the Tuscan, Filippo Buonaccorsi, also known as Callimachus and to Conrad Celtes, founder of Sodalitas Litteraria Vistulana.

The fifteenth century was not renowned for many large-scale architectural monuments. Basically, the large churches originating from the previous century were finished, decorated and fortifications were developed. The years 1498-1499 brought the most impressive defence structure, the Barbican, the artillery stronghold protecting the Floriańska Gate and the Town Arsenal. The view of the late mediaeval Cracow can be seen in its oldest presentation - a woodcut, in the Hartmann Schedel's "The Chronicle of the World", published in Nuremberg in 1493.

The fifteenth century is however the period in which late Gothic sculpture and painting flourished. Starting from the end of 14th century the majority of Cracow's carving shops were producing wooden sculptures. The earliest sculptures were single statues, being eventually grouped in box type altars, which around mid -15th century took a classical shape of a polyptych with folding side wings. Many late Gothic altars combined the elements of sculpture and painting which along with the techniques shared by both fields of art, contributed to their parallel stylistic development. The fine art of the late 14th century tended to idealise figures and use elegant, decorative presentation of soft draperies. This feature earned it the name of "soft" style, and its early fifteenth century phase was known as "bella maniera". The examples include the most beautiful, full of courtly elegance Madonnas of Cracow, with the famous sculpture found in Krużlowa (approx. 1410). Furthermore, the oldest panel paintings such as the Epitaph of Wierzbięta of

Branice which dates from around 1425.

The years 1440-1470 brought a crisis in the painting and sculpture of the Lesser Poland and are known as the "dark" period. There are only a few examples left and their stylistic expression is difficult to determine. This phenomenon was related to the gradual embracing by the Cracow artists of new trends from the West, consisting in increasingly realistic treatment of objects and specific stylization of draperies. Soft draperies were replaced with angular forms as if made of metal plate or cardboard. The birth process of the new "angular" style is best illustrated by the paintings and sculptures of the retables adorning the Holy Cross Chapel in the Cathedral - "The Holy Trinity" triptych of 1476 and the "Our Lady of the Sorrows" triptych dating 1475-1480, as well as the paintings of the Augustian polyptych by Nicholas Haberschack (1468).

The triumph of naturalism and dramatic expression in the final phase of Gothic art in Cracow is closely related to Veit Stoss. In the years of 1477- 1489 he created the high altar of Our Lady's Church, one of the most magnificent altars of this type in Europe and one of the most precious works of art in Poland. Of equally high artistic value is his stone crucifix in the same church and the tomb of Casimir Jagiellon in the Cathedral. Arguably there was no artist among the Cracow painters whose talent could match that of Veit Stoss. The paintings produced by the Cracow artists of that time are the polyptych of Olkusz by Jan Wielki and Stanisław Stary. The paintings of the Książnice polyptych made by Michael the Painter in 1491 resemble that of Stoss to the extent that there were attempts to attribute them to him. Apart from painters specialising in panel paintings there were some artists in Cracow who excelled in miniatures illuminating magnificent parchment codexes.

The style introduced by Veit Stoss dominated the painting and sculpture of Cracow for generations, though after his return to Nuremberg in 1496, a tendency appeared to quench the dynamics and expression. After 1500, a notable deterioration of the decorative art level was observed, as it clearly did not manage to meet the challenges of the modern times.

Apart from sculpture and painting, the late Gothic in Cracow left splendid specimens of artistic craft, mainly goldsmithery and embroidery. The most eminent goldsmith was Marcin Marciniec whose work included the richly ornamented reliquary for the head of St. Stanislaus made in 1504 and currently kept in the Cathedral Treasury.

Casimir Jagiellon died in 1492, the year America was discovered, after 45 years on the throne – the longest rule in the history of Poland. His successors, John Albert (Jan Olbracht) and Alexander died young. In 1506, the youngest

son of Casimir, Sigismund, later called the Old, began his reign which was to last over forty years. Neither he nor any of his contemporaries realised that during the several, rather unstable years since his father's death, Poland not only underwent transformations which were to determine its political system for the following three hundred years but that the big hand on the clock of history crossed the dividing line between the Middle Ages and the modern times. Poland at the beginning of the 16th century had already elected monarchs with limited powers and its noblemen were holding the monopoly of political rights. The new political system was much more inconvenient for towns and they inevitably approached some crisis which was as yet difficult to determine. There came however a real revolution in the field of culture. The artistic undertakings of the royal court at the beginning of the 16th century introduced Renaissance art to Cracow in Italian form. The northern, Gothic City of Cracow became a colony of classical Mediterranean culture.

One of the essential factors in the development of Cracow in the late Middle Ages was its function as the capital of the country. This function continued throughout the whole of the 16th century but Cracow's location far from the centre of the enormous country was becoming increasingly inconvenient. The Sejm (Parliament) was mostly convened in Piotrków, and since 1569 in Warsaw which gradually acquired more and more prerogatives of a capital city. In 1609 King Sigismund III Vasa left Cracow for the Moscow War. On returning, he settled in Warsaw, which since that moment begun its history as the state capital. Cracow had to be satisfied with the status of capital de jure and the place where rulers were crowned and buried. As it soon appeared, these honours were not sufficient to maintain the town's prosperity for a long period of time. The population of Cracow nevertheless kept growing and reached about 20 thousands towards the end of the sixteenth century. This number declined only after the great plague in 1651 and the Swedish invasion four years later. The German element which until this period had dominated, was undergoing fast polonisation. The overt sign of this change was the transferring, in 1537, of German sermons from Our Lady's Church to the much smaller St. Barbara's. There was however a strong wave of immigration from Italy. The Italians living in Cracow dealt mainly with finances and trade but some of them were artists to whom the town owes its Renaissance characteristics. It is worth remembering that the Italians - Prosper Provano and Sebastian Montelupi were the founders of the first permanent Polish postal system.

The 16th and the first half of the 17th century still witnessed prosperity of Cracow though its structural foundations grew increasingly weaker. The eastern trading route lost its

importance when the Turks started to occupy the Black Sea coasts and trade with the east was dominated by Lvov. Also the trade power of Gdańsk partly cut off Cracow's contacts with the West. The political system favouring nobility and their main occupation - farming, hindered transition to new production relations based on capital even though Cracow was predisposed to become a modern industrial centre like Nuremberg or Augsburg. The measure of a burgher's success was not so much winning the fortune based on manufacture or trade but through ennobling and embracing the land owners lifestyle. In this way the city kept losing its most gifted and most energetic citizens.

The burgher community of Cracow was rather conservative and largely untouched by the Reformation. Protestantism was officially recognised as late as 1552, which is why Cracow was spared the fights and cultural losses connected with religious controversies. The hardly noticeable Reformation movement in the town was however a reflection of its weakening ties with the West and in particular with Germany, which had been very strong in the 15th and at the beginning of the 16th century.

The University was gradually losing the importance it had held in the late Middle Ages. The number of students decreased and the University was becoming markedly confined to the traditional organisation and scholastic tradition. It does not however change the fact that in the 16th and even at the beginning of the 17th century eminent professors such as Sebastian Petrycy and Jan Brożek worked for the University. Among the students were such luminaries of Polish culture as a poet, Jan Kochanowski and a writer, Andrzej Frycz Modrzewski.

The centre of cultural life and artistic patronage was the royal court of the last kings of the Jagiellonian dynasty. Poles prevailed among the humanists related to the court. They were mostly clergymen educated in Italian universities, using classical Latin and laying the foundations of literature in the Polish language.

The Humanist literary movement found a valuable base in the Cracow printing houses of Ungler, Wietor, Łazarz, Andrysowicz, Wierzbięta, the Siebeneichers, the Scharffenbergs and the Piotrkowczyks. They printed the works of Długosz's successors - Maciej Miechowita, Marcin Kromer, Marcin Bielski and Aleksander Gwagnin, and their books, apart from containing precious information of all kinds, reveal the oldest illustrations of various events from the history of Poland.

Royal patronage prompted an early, on the European scale, introduction of the Italian Renaissance art to Poland.

The beginning was given by Francesco Fiorentino who made John Albert's tomb in the Cathedral in the years 1502-1504. His art was also decisive in the shape of Renaissance

architectural elements of Wawel Castle. The most renowned artist of the early phase of the Renaissance in Poland was Bartolomeo Berecci, the creator of the Sigismund Chapel (1519 - 1531). This gave rise to the countless number of mausoleums and noblemen's tombs scattered all over the country.

The Renaissance forms in the town first appeared in the residences of the higher clergy at Kanonicza Street, which resembled small palaces with arcaded courtyards. In the years 1556-1560 the Cloth Hall was remodelled, receiving its impressive parapet decorated with mascarons most probably by Santi Gucci and the Renaissance loggias to which Giovanni Maria Mosca, also known as Padovano, greatly contributed. Renaissance style reached Cracow in its classic Tuscan-Roman version. Around the middle of the 16th century appeared decorative and expressive examples of mannerism, whilst Netherlandish influences were also gradually growing.

This kind of art dominated entirely the so called small architectural forms, especially tombs. The greatest number of this kind of monument can be found in the Cathedral, in Our Lady's Church and in the ambulatory of the Dominican Monastery. At first, the new architecture and sculpture were the exclusive domain of the Italians. Only in the 1670's did a Polish artist fully grasped the principles of Renaissance art. It was Jan Michałowicz of Urzędów whose main work is the Bishop Padniewski's Chapel in the Cathedral.

The situation of painting was quite different. Italian representatives of this discipline rarely visited 16th century Cracow. The only recognised major work of an Italian Renaissance painter working in Cracow is, "The Crucifixion" by Pietro Veneziano from the old high altar of the Cathedral, which can be now found in the church in Bodzentyn. The local artistic community, was relatively strong combining the still popular tradition of Gothic painting with the modern awareness of three dimensional space and the Renaissance ornaments and forms. The best known representatives of this approach were Jerzy and, primarily, Stanisław Samostrzelnik (mentioned in the sources in 1506-1541), a Cistercian monk from Mogiła. An excellent painter of miniatures but also the author of murals and most probably also portraits.

They resemble Northern Renaissance, mostly German painting. Cracow also hosted eminent representatives of the Franconian school: Michael Lancz of Kitzingen and Hans Dürer, a brother of the famous Albrecht. The recent conservation of the strip in the Tournament Hall of Wawel Castle allowed to bring a well grounded hypothesis concerning the parts of ornaments made by him. Moreover, numerous works of Hans Suess of Kulmbach which were made in Cracow constitute an indirect evidence proving his presence in the town approximately between 1514-1516. In the 16th century first portraits appeared in the Polish

painting tradition. Its development was mainly influenced by the portraits of kings and bishops adorning the ambulatory of the Franciscan Monastery.

The Cracow decorative art - goldsmithery and other metal working techniques, embroidery, weaving etc. continued the Gothic traditions throughout the whole 16th century. It should also be noted that the majority of gold objects founded by Sigismund the Old were also Gothic in nature. In many cases the most beautiful works of decorative art ordered by the King were foreign imports. This was the case for the decorative objects for the Sigismund Chapel which were imports from Nuremberg and the impressive collection of tapestries ordered by Sigismund Augustus from the best workshops in Brussels.

Concluding, the art of 16th century Cracow is not homogenous and contrary to the previous century, lacks a continuous line of development. Renaissance enriched it with new, valuable assets but at the same time the local artists were faced with challenges that they were unable to confront. The guild structure of training and organisation of artistic work made it impossible for the local artists-craftsmen to follow the development of European art, which in turn offered many opportunities to the visitors from abroad. This condition was to last until as late as the 19th century.

Sigismund III's departure from Cracow in 1609, the great plague of 1651 and finally the Swedish invasion filled the history of Cracow in the 17th century as it plummeted towards a deepening crisis. This tendency could not be reversed by magnificent events such as coronations and ceremonial inaugurations of monarchs. The Swedish occupation during 1655-1657 left Cracow with losses the town did not recover from for until the late 18th century. The number of inhabitants dropped dramatically and hardly reached 10 thousand by the beginning of the 18th century. Economic life was reduced to the level of local manufacturing and trade. The town fortifications were gradually falling into ruin. When the court left Cracow, the town no longer attracted the ruling elite. The palaces and manor houses of the aristocracy and rich noblemen were, one by one, given to convents.

This last fact, evidence of the crisis the town was experiencing, does not however correspond to the similar scale downfall of art in 17th century Cracow. Though weakened, the country still had considerable resources and the atmosphere of Counter-Reformation prompted generous donations to the Church. Therefore, unlike the 16th , the 17th century was the period of new, often monumental churches and of large scale modernisation of the interiors of mediaeval churches.

This series of important religious foundations is reflected in

the opening of the Jesuit Church of St. Peter and St. Paul at Grodzka Street, already started by the end of the 16th century. Historians are not in agreement over the history of its foundation and the names of the artists involved. The available sources reveal that the final shape was given to the church by Giovanni Trevano in 1609 - 1619. The church is closely related to the architecture of Rome and was modelled on the main Jesuit sanctuary - the *Il Gesù* in Rome. It is a monumental structure - a little austere but at the same time full of courtly elegance. The style perfectly corresponds to the nature of the Counter-Reformation period which the Jesuits served so well, and to the ideas which were shared by the founder - king Sigismund III. Of particular beauty is the stone laid façade, and the stucco interior decoration reflecting the programme of unity of eastern and western Christianity, of special significance at that time.

Of no inferior artistic value is the Calmedolite Church in the suburb of Bielany, built in two phases between 1609 - 1630. The founder of the Calmedolite hermitage was the Crown Marshall Mikołaj Wolski. He brought the design from Rome and the church was later built to this design most probably by Walenty von Sabisch. The façade is believed to have been designed by Andrea Spezza. In this case we deal with architecture achieving the effect of monumentality and elegance using very simple means. The splendour of the church, and in particular of the stone façade framed with two towers, is in contrast with the extremely strict rules of the Calmedolite order.

The majority of 17th century Cracow churches are architecturally inferior to the genuinely European achievements represented by the above described Jesuit and Calmedolite churches. Outstanding for its size and space is the Bernardine Church in Stradom, built by Krzysztof Mieroszewski, an architect and military engineer, in 1670-1680. Characteristic features of this structure comprise of towers in the façade modelled on *Il Gesù* with the dome submerged in the roof. This was required to allow unobstructed shelling from the canons stationed at the neighbouring Wawel Castle. Of interest is also the Visitant Church in Krowoderska Street (the former bishops' jurisdiction), built in 1686-1695. Apart from quality architecture the church also presents uniform interior arrangement from the end of the 17th century. The whole monastery constitutes a fascinating living fossil of the three hundred years old construction in the heart of a modern city.

While the religious architecture of 17th century Cracow began with strong features represented by the Church of St. Peter and St. Paul and the Calmedolite Church, it ended with a work of equal, if not higher standing - St. Anne's Church.

Since the 15th century the church belonged to the University. Towards the end of the 17th century, the University, though the days of its glory were past, decided to attempt a new and much more splendid foundation. The main role here was played by the prestige factors - competition with the Jesuits who intended to monopolise the whole education system as well as the growing cult of John of Kanti (Jan Kanty) who was soon to become a saint. The new church was built in 1689-1703 according to the design of Tylman van Gameren, the best architect then active in Poland, representing the classicism oriented branch of Baroque. In accordance with the wish of the University authorities, the layout of the building is modelled on the San Andrea della Valle Church in Rome, another example of the *Il Gesù* type. The church was given a two towered façade in consideration of the view from the narrow street.

The magnificent stucco interior decoration is the work of Baldassare Fontana, an Italian coming from near the Swiss border. He brought to Cracow the Baroque sculpture originating directly from the circle of Gianlorenzo Bernini. Fontana was also an architect and designed some elements of the sacral architecture. The interior of St. Anne's presents one of the best examples in Poland of the Baroque combination of all artistic domains. Other than architecture and sculpture, it also contains high quality paintings by Karol Dankwart and Innocenty and Karol Monti. This polyphonic decoration illustrates a complex theological programme that was most probably worked out by Rev. Sebastian Piskorski, one of the University professors, amateur architect and supervisor of the church erection works.

Apart from churches, mausoleum chapels continued to be built. The leading achievements in this field were the Zbaraski Chapel in the Dominican Church, dating from 1627-1633, attributed to Constantin Tencalla and the Vasa Chapel in the Cathedral. This was completed in 1676 and is, from the outside, an exact copy of the Sigismund Chapel.

As far as secular architecture is concerned, the 17th century began with reconstruction of the northern wing of Wawel Castle during 1599 - 1603 by Giovanni Trevano under the order of Sigismund III. At that time the Senators' Staircase was built with its course broken between floors, and monumental ornamentation. This very well fitted the stiff Spanish etiquette adopted at the court of the first Polish king of the Vasa dynasty. Similar staircases, a novelty in Polish architecture, were gradually introduced in urban residences remodelled in the Baroque style. A good example of such staircases can be found in Krzysztofory Palace.

The 17th century filled the interiors of the Cracow churches with a great number of new altars, stalls and other furnishings.

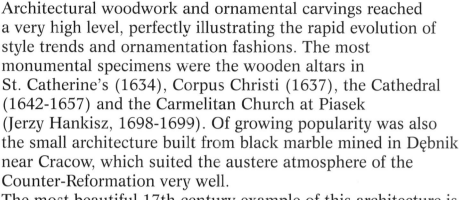

Architectural woodwork and ornamental carvings reached a very high level, perfectly illustrating the rapid evolution of style trends and ornamentation fashions. The most monumental specimens were the wooden altars in St. Catherine's (1634), Corpus Christi (1637), the Cathedral (1642-1657) and the Carmelitan Church at Piasek (Jerzy Hankisz, 1698-1699). Of growing popularity was also the small architecture built from black marble mined in Dębnik near Cracow, which suited the austere atmosphere of the Counter-Reformation very well.

The most beautiful 17th century example of this architecture is the Calced Carmelites Church altar at Kopernika Street. The figural sculpture was much less impressive, though Sebastian Gala and Giovanni Francesco de Rossi worked in Cracow at that time. This domain of art reached its highest level at the end of the century thanks to Baldassare Fontana. Beside St. Anne's he also decorated St. Andrew's Church, St. Hyacynth's Chapel in the Dominican Church and a number of secular interiors.

Seventeenth century Cracow painting did not produce any great masterpieces. In the first half of the century it was dominated by a Venetian - Tommaso Dolabella, the artist of, among others, large biblical paintings in the Dominican Church. A Bernardine monk, Franciszek Lekszycki, decorated the church of his order with large altar paintings, most of them being copies of Rubens and Van Dyck's compositions.

The eighteenth century is known as the period of the deepest decline of Cracow. At the beginning of the century the town was invaded by repeated Swedish occupations which brought about contributions, robberies and the disastrous fire of Wawel Castle.

Further, though not as extensive damage occurred during the Succession War (1733-1735) and the Seven Year -War (1756-1763). In 1768, Cracow became one of the centres of an anti-Russian (Barska) Confederation which it paid for with a siege and a four-year Russian occupation. There were very few brighter points in the life of the town. The coronation of Augustus III in 1734 was a truly baroque ceremony with magnificent artistic program but the last king of Poland, Stanislaus Augustus Poniatowski, was crowned in Warsaw, depriving the old capital of one of its last prerogatives. The last monumental ceremony took place in Cracow in 1775 on the occassion of the canonization of John of Kanti.

The economic situation of the town was rapidly deteriorating, and as a result of the first partition of Poland it was cut off by the border from its natural base and market in the Subcarpathian area and in Ruthenia. Some attempts to improve the situation came with the Enlightenment period and

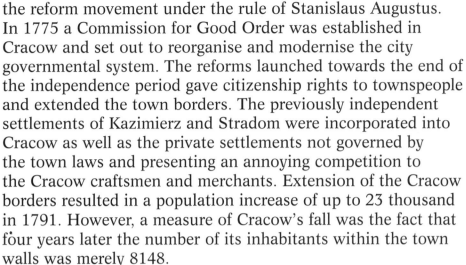

the reform movement under the rule of Stanislaus Augustus. In 1775 a Commission for Good Order was established in Cracow and set out to reorganise and modernise the city governmental system. The reforms launched towards the end of the independence period gave citizenship rights to townspeople and extended the town borders. The previously independent settlements of Kazimierz and Stradom were incorporated into Cracow as well as the private settlements not governed by the town laws and presenting an annoying competition to the Cracow craftsmen and merchants. Extension of the Cracow borders resulted in a population increase of up to 23 thousand in 1791. However, a measure of Cracow's fall was the fact that four years later the number of its inhabitants within the town walls was merely 8148.

In the intellectual sphere, a great event was the reform of the University implemented by Hugo Kołłłątaj and Jan Sniadecki in 1780. Following the ideas of the Enlightenment, special attention was given to sciences and the University obtained an astronomical observatory, a hospital and a botanical garden. In 1781 the first theatre was opened in Cracow which gave performances in the Polish language. The above described events were accompanied by a certain economic revival. Patriotic awareness was also growing and its culmination point was the Oath taken by Tadeusz Kościuszko in the Market Square on 24th March 1794. The reformatory processes were broken by the fall of the uprising, the Prussian occupation and finally, the incorporation of Cracow into the territory of Austria in January 1796.

Despite the aforementioned desperate condition of Cracow, in the 18th century the town continued to acquire notable works of art. Of primary importance was late Baroque architecture, with Kasper Bażanka and Francesco Placidi as its leading representatives. Bażanka graduated at St. Lucas Academy in Rome and his works were often influenced by the architecture of the Eternal City. In the Missionaries' Church in Stradom Street (built 1719-1728) he blended the designs close to those used in the interior of the Three Magi Chapel at the Palace of Congregation for Spreading Faith by Francesco Borromini and façade drawing on St. Andrew's Church, in Rome, by Gianlorenzo Bernini. The typically Baroque trick of correcting the reality by perspective illusion is exemplified by the wall in front of the Church of St. Peter and St. Paul (built in 1715-1722). The wall conceals the fact that the façade is out of line with Grodzka Street.

Placidi was born a Roman but his style was also influenced by his Dresden years. His works count among the most significant achievements of late Baroque architecture in Poland. Placidi's principal works in Cracow are the Trinitarian Church (now Good Friars) in Kazimierz (1752-1758) and the Piarist

Church façade (1759-1761). The church itself was designed by Bażanka (1718-1728). In these structures he showed excellent understanding of urban conditions in relation to architecture. In both cases he used façades of similar planimetric model which originated from the *Il Gesù* type, enriched with an additional vertical element. The Piarist façade at the end of Św.Jana Street is meant to be viewed from the front. It is flat, its cuts forming a decorative outline against the sky, while the façade of the Trinitarian Church, viewed from the side, is wavy and closed on the top with a three dimensional turret. Placidi also showed late Baroque architectural skills in reconstructing the Lipski Family Chapel in the Cathedral in 1743-1746. Windows hidden in the miniature presbytery provide a dramatic illumination of the altar.

A monumental artistic undertaking was the building of a new Pauline Church at Skałka carried out in the years 1734-1742 by Jerzy Muntzer and Antonio Solari. The façade of the church, adorned with two towers, is an important element in the panorama of Cracow seen from the Vistula bank. The classicist phase of 18th century architecture is more modest than Baroque. It relates to the reconstruction of St. Norbert's Church in Zwierzyniec built in 1777 to the design of Rev. Sebastian Sierakowski. Good examples of classicist residences are the façades of the Wodzicki Family palaces in the Main Market Square (1777-1783), later owned by the Potocki Family, and in Św. Jana Street, attributed to Ferdynand Nax. Felix Radwański built new university buildings: Collegium Phisicum at Św. Anny Street (the present Kołłątaj Collegium) and the astronomical observatory in the former Wesoła suburb (1784-1788), with the contribution of Stanisław Zawadzki).

Eighteenth century sculpture in Cracow starts with the works of David Heel, a Jesuit artist who made the statues on the façade of St. Peter's and St. Paul's and on the wall in front of this church. The stylistic expression of this domain of art was mainly shaped by the outstanding heritage of Baldassare Fontana. Antoni Frączkiewicz, active in the years 1715-1741, a skilful craftsman but lacking any talent for original composition, often copied in wood the stucco figures by Fontana. His works can be found, among others, in the Missionaries' Church in Stradom and in the Calmedolite Church in Bielany. The Pauline Church at Skałka was decorated by Johan Georg Lehner who came from the Silesian-Moravian border and the much less gifted Wojciech Rojowski. It appears that the best Cracow sculptor of the end of the century was Antoni Gugenpauer, drawing in many ways on the then dominant Lvov school of sculpture. His elongated, graceful statues adorn the altars of Bernardine and Corpus Christi churches. A monumental, but not very successful

example of neo-classical sculpture is the tomb of Bishop Kajetan Sołtyk in the Cathedral, designed by Rev. Sebastian Sierakowski.

Cracow art in he 18th century is considerably rich and diverse. The town was visited by the leading Polish painters, educated in Rome - Szymon Czechowicz and Tadeusz Kuntze (Konicz). The interiors of new churches were commonly covered with fresco decorations. In the Piarist Church the decoration was made by Franz Eckstein and co-workers (1733) and in the Trinitarian Church - by Joseph Piltz. Both painters came from Moravia, such as the above mentioned Lehner and numerous artists of various specialities then working in Poland. It should finally be mentioned that in 1747, painters in Cracow managed to free themselves from the restraints of the guilds. They came under the protection of the University, thus making the first step towards obtaining the status of a modern artist.

When Cracow was incorporated into Austria, paradoxically enough it regained contact with its natural hinterland across the Vistula River. That, together with relations with the more advanced provinces of the Hapsburg monarchy led to some economical revival of the town. It was not Cracow however that became the capital of Galicia, because this function was taken by Lvov from1772. With time, this was to cause the unequal development of both cities in the 19th century. Cracow lost its local government, replaced by far reaching centralisation and extensive police system. German was used in the institutions and at the University. On the other side however, the Austrian authorities began to clean up and modernise the hopelessly run down city. Some of these projects were desperately needed - like the liquidation of the small church cemeteries and foundation of the Rakowice Cemetery. Other actions, intended to facilitate the extension of the city area, led to destruction of numerous historical buildings including medieval churches and to gradual pulling down of the defence walls.

After the defeat of Austria in 1807 Cracow joined the Duchy of Warsaw which, apart from patriotic connotations, meant the implementation of the Napoleonic Code and free trade privileges for the city. This was unfortunately only a short interval. The Congress of Vienna in 1815 created the miniature Republic of Cracow which consisted of the city and its environs and was under the auspices of the three partitioning powers. This solution was obviously better than direct incorporation into Austria because it offered an additional forty years of existence of a limited but Polish by nature state, not to speak about freedom of cultural development.

The Republic of Cracow was 1164 square kilometres and its

population from the original 88 thousand grew up to 146 thousand in 1842. The population of Cracow itself grew from 23 to 43 thousand respectively. The Constitution of 1815 and 1818 was relatively liberal. Power was in the hands of the Parliament (the Representative Assembly) and the government called Ruling Senate. Due to the census system, political power belonged to landowners and wealthy townspeople, but there were also representatives of the peasants. The University could also delegate its representative to the Senate.

The status of a free city located at the junction of three superpower states ensured a relatively good economic performance. It related both to the city and to the surrounding villages whose level of development was much higher than that of neighbouring Galicia and parts of Poland under Russian rule. Cracow was being systematically modernised. A sewage system was built, most streets were paved and buildings were repaired. In place of the nearly totally demolished defence walls a beautiful park called "Planty" was set up. In 1844 construction of a railway track leading westwards was started, and the first train reached Cracow in 1847.

At least officially free from the foreign oppression, Cracow was gradually assuming the role of the centre of Polish spirit. Romantic patriotism, a cult of heroism and history gave a start to a specific Cracow custom of commemorating distinguished people. The ceremonial funerals of Prince Józef Poniatowski (1817) and Tadeusz Kościuszko (1818), who were laid to rest in the royal crypts of the Cathedral, made people think of the crypts as a national pantheon. In 1820-1823 the Kościuszko Mound was raised, in the style of prehistoric mounds of Krakus and Wanda. Romantic research of the country's past was developing with its first representative - Ambroży Grabowski, the author of "A Historical Description of the City of Cracow", dated 1822.

Cracow did not join the November Uprising of 1830-1831 but paid for support offered to the fighters with the Russian occupation in 1831. After the fall of the Uprising, numerous refugees started coming from the Russian occupied parts of Poland. They continued patriotic activity in Cracow which in turn brought about another occupation, this time by the Austrian army, in 1836-1841. The Polish patriotic circles did not give in. In February 1846 an uprising broke up in Cracow but it fell due to the blood bath of the peasant rebellion against the noblemen. After the patriotic forces were crushed at Gdów, Russian and Austrian troops entered the city and soon the Republic was annexed to Austria.

The achievements of Cracow culture and the art of the first part of the 19th century are very modest. The University was regaining its Polish character. The Academic Society of Cracow

was founded in 1816 and the School of Fine Arts was founded in 1818. They were to develop later into The Academy of Arts and Sciences and the Academy of Fine Arts, which greatly contributed to the Polish culture of the 19th and 20th centuries. The theatre was located in the building in the Szczepański Square, which now houses the Stary Theatre, extended in 1842 by Karol Kremer.

Building projects in the Republic of Cracow were extremely few. The situation was a little better in the domain of painting. The beginning of the century brought the works of Michał Stachowicz, whose poor but historically valuable presentations of important events and the city life were filled with romantic patriotism. Jan Peszka painted good portraits and Jan Nepomucen Głowacki set foundations for Polish landscape paintings. Wojciech Korneli Stattler undertook an ambitious program of creating a monumental national allegory suggested by Adam Mickiewicz. Still, his main works of art did not manage to rise above conventional classicist standards.

An excellent painter was Piotr Michałowski, closely linked to French Romanticism. A rich landowner and a politician , he painted his realistic battles, scenic views, portraits and animals mostly for himself and close friends and relatives. He did not teach painting, never sold or exhibited his works in public, he even refused to accept chairmanship of the Society of Friends to Fine Arts, so his truly European art was nearly unknown in the provincial Cracow.

The period of about seventy years which passed from annexing Cracow to Austria to the outbreak of the First World War and regaining independence, splits into two opposing phases. The first, that lasted until 1867 was extremely difficult for the city. It was deprived of the liberal system of the Republic and the Germanization pressure was restored. In April 1948 Cracow was bombed to quench the patriotic rebellion on the wave of the Spring of the Nations. The January Uprising of 1863 did not involve Galicia but the attempts to offer assistance resulted in severe repressions.

At the same time, the situation of Galicia and Cracow was slowly improving. Already in the years 1859 - 1861 Parliaments were called for respective lands of the Empire, and the city autonomy was restored. The new City Council of Cracow was headed by a perfect organiser, Dr. Józef Dietl. Full democracy and autonomy was brought by the Austrian Constitution of 1867. Cracow soon became the centre of political movement grouped around the "Czas" daily which combined patriotism with promoting systematic efforts in political, economic and educational work. The "Stańczyks" party named after their ideological manifesto referring to the 16th century royal jester, dominated in Cracow until the end of the 19th century.

The autonomy allowed to start extensive works on modernisation of the city. A succession of urban reforms followed and the former suburbs became incorporated into the city. The beginning of the 19th century witnessed the onset of the so called Greater Cracow of the area of 47 square kilometres, nearly ten times bigger than only 40 years before. Population grew from 50 thousand in 1869 to 180 thousand in 1915. Modern facilities were gradually introduced - gas and electricity systems, generally accessible water supply and sewerage, finally - horse drawn and later electric trams.

The development continued though there was practically no modern industry. It was based on the growing part of Cracow as the Polish cultural centre, trade and a large Austrian garrison stationed in Cracow as a border stronghold.

This development gave birth to a vivid construction movement. The public and private buildings in their scale and quality reflect the modest means of the Cracow investors and are by far inferior to the architecture of Warsaw or Lvov. Until the 1890's the obligatory convention was Historicism with special preference to neo-Renaissance. The source of this inspiration was Vienna and the local historical buildings. Examples of this trend are The School of Fine Arts at Matejko Square (Maciej Moraczewski, 1880) and the Słowacki Theatre (Jan Zawieyski, 1893). Towards the end of the century one of the most interesting architects was Teodor Talowski who built a number of romantic full of fantasy buildings along Retoryka Street which combined mediaeval style and Mannerism. The turn of the century brought the Art Nouveau style usually joined with historic elements. The best example of the architecture of this time is Szczepański Square with the Fine Arts Society building (Franciszek Mączyński, 1901) and the façade of the Stary Theatre remodelled, in 1903-1906 by Franciszek Mączyński and Tadeusz Stryjeński. Around 1910 Art Nouveau was replaced by a simplified, geometric phase of Modernism represented, for example, by the Technology and Industry Museum in Smoleńsk Street (Tadeusz Stryjeński, Józef Czajkowski, 1908-1914) and the School of Industry in Mickiewicza Alley (Sławomir Odrzywolski, 1912). Rapid changes of architectural styles were accompanied by new technologies - like reinforced concrete, and modern facilities - central heating and lifts.

The liberal conditions in Galicia of that time led to fast development of cultural life in Cracow. The University started to flourish again. The Academy of Arts and Sciences, founded in 1873, became the most prestigious corporation of scholars in the whole of Poland. In 1876 Cracow got its first public museum - the Czartoryski Collection. The National Museum was founded in 1883 and soon came into possession of valuable collections of mediaeval art and 19th century Polish paintings.

After a period of demolition of old buildings in the first half of the 19th century came modern awareness of the value of historical monuments. Numerous conservation projects began and were carried out with deep respect for the historical heritage. Performing the restoration works in the Cathedral, Sławomir Odrzywolski did not change its character of a unique conglomerate of styles. Though Tadeusz Stryjeński, removed the Baroque interior decorations while renovating Our Lady's Church, he preserved valuable 18th century altars and other precious old elements. If new features were introduced to historical buildings they were basically of high artistic value, like Jan Matejko's murals in Our Lady's Church or Stanisław Wyspiański's polychromy and stained glass windows in the Franciscan Church. There were also unfortunate mistakes like the demolition of the mediaeval Holy Spirit Church and hospital complex, the project unsuccessfully opposed by Matejko. An important expression of the specific cult of the past was the foundation in 1898 of the Society of Lovers of Cracow History and Ancient Buildings, which still promotes historical awareness and inspires research work.

In the second half of the 19th century Cracow's position as the capital of the divided country was restored, not formally but spiritually. The tradition of the "national monument city" was continued by organisation of grandiose historical and patriotic celebrations. Examples include, the reburial of King Casimir the Great (1869), the bringing of the ashes of Adam Mickiewicz from France (1890) and the 500th anniversary of the Battle of Grunwald (1910). Thanks to Jan Matejko and the Art School known since 1900 as the Academy of Fine Arts, Cracow also became the artistic capital of Poland for about half a century. Matejko was both one of the main founders and the product of the Cracow Historism. His monumental works were inspired by the past but the artist addressed his contemporaries, trying to show them the way to the long lost glory. Matejko did not live to see an independent homeland but the Poles rewarded his efforts offering him in 1878 a sceptre which symbolised his spiritual rule of the Polish art. A still greater reward to the artist was the fact that a great many Poles still see the past of their country in the form given to it by Matejko in his "The Battle of Grunwald", " The Prussian Tribute" and "The Lublin Union". Of Matejko's generation was also another painter, Aleksander Kotsis, the author of rural scenes. Juliusz Kossak, an immensely popular author of well known paintings, also spent the last years of his life in Cracow. Matejko's phenomenon vastly influences Polish art, and more generally, Polish culture. As long-time director of the School of Fine Arts he brought the School to a very high level of artistic performance. Feeding the love of history to his students he did not however suppress their individuality or halt their

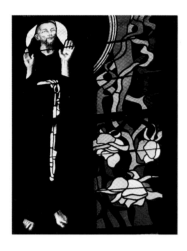

development. Among his students counted the most prominent representatives of Polish Modernism - Jacek Malczewski, Stanisław Wyspiański and Józef Mehoffer. Soon after Matejko's death in the mid-nineties, the traditional and immersed in history Cracow gave rise to the modernist trend known as Young Poland. Jan Fałat became the director of the School of Fine Arts starting extensive reforms. In 1897 the "Sztuka" (Art) Society was established, active in propagating new ideas. The artistic circles were led by the demonic Stanisław Przybyszewski whose motto was "art for art's sake", a negation of the former objective of art treated as service to the nation. New forms of artistic life and expression appeared. Literary and artistic publications and the artistic cabaret "Zielony Balonik" flourished. The interior of the "Jama Michalika" cafe where the cabaret performances were held belongs to the most valuable phenomena in the culture of Young Poland.

The twenty years between 1895 and 1914 bring the greatest abundance and most extensive development of Polish painting. Centred around The Academy of Fine Arts was a group of leading artists such as Julian Fałat, Leon Wyczółkowski, Jacek Malczewski, Stanisław Wyspiański, Józef Mehoffer, Jan Stanisławski, Józef Pankiewicz and Wojciech Weiss. The art of each of them is different but together they make an impressive panorama of the century's art, not only representing unsurpassed richness and beauty but also homogeneity of their style. The artistic and intellectual problems of the turn of century were best expressed by Jacek Malczewski and Stanisław Wyspiański. The first of them, perhaps the most popular Polish painter, created compositions full of individual symbolism. These referred to the basic problems of life and death, specifically to the artist's life, and what is important, to the still hot issue of regaining independence. Stanisław Wyspiański was a versatile genius, presenting his ideas with equal ease in various painting techniques, poetry and drama. His art was a conscious continuation of romantic poetry and Matejko's painting tradition but it often contradicted its sources. In his dramas and in particular in his most popular "Wesele" Wyspiański took up the problem of the national fight for independence on an unprecedented scale. In his paintings he combined historical and folk inspirations using decorative and expressive forms. His stained glass windows, both those actually made of glass and those that remained as designs, rank among the highest achievements of modern European sacral art.

The *fin de siècle* period, full of colour and charm, lasted in Cracow till 1914. The outbreak of the First World War revealed that the city, known for academic and artistic achievements, was also home to serious political and military ideas aimed at

reconstitution of the independent state. On 6th August 1914, a few hours before the official start of the War between Austria and Russia, the famous first battalion of the paramilitary organisation called "Strzelec" under the command of Józef Piłsudski crossed the border of the part of Poland occupied by Russia, starting an almost private war with the chief occupant. The Romantic undertaking, though it resembled that of 1863, was successful this time. Soon the Polish Legions were called up under the aegis of the Supreme National Committee, which became the core of the future Polish army. The war did not directly affect Cracow though the front line stopped several kilometres from the city. When the fronts became stabilised, despite all the austerities, fairly normal life returned to the city. The University was again active, annual patriotic ceremonies were organised and even conservation works were carried out at the Wawel Hill. In autumn 1918 the much-awaited independence was very close. On 31st October the Austrian contingent in Cracow was disarmed and the Austrian Imperial insignia removed. The War was officially going on but the former capital of Poland was free - as the first of Polish cities.

Between the World Wars, Cracow had the status of a city of intellectuals and scholars situated slightly away from the centre of the country's mainstream. It could longer aspire to the role of a capital city, even in a spiritual and cultural sense. Having however a fifty-year experience of autonomy and the eminent University it played an important role in providing specialists for political life, administration and army. Population rose to 250 thousand in 1939. The city grew within the borderlines established by the Greater Cracow project from 1915. A cultural and academic quarter was created along Mickiewicz Avenue, with the monumental structures of the Academy of Mining (Wacław Krzyżanowski, completed in 1939), the National Museum (Czesław Boratyński, Edward Kreisiler, B.Schmidt) and the Jagiellonian Library (Wacław Krzyżanowski, 1937-1939). Typical for the period were villas best exampled by the so-called "Osiedle Oficerskie" quarter. Apart from Classicist traditions persisting until the Second World War, architectural preferences were expressed in the strictly functional manner. The buildings consisted of simplified shapes and façades decorated with emblems, which were in agreement with the Cracow tradition and building regulations. Despite the change of political situation, patriotic celebrations continued which are best exampled by rising the mound to Marshal Piłsudski at the top of the Sowiniec Hill. In the arts, the great traditions of the Young Poland were alive. Still active were Malczewski, Fałat, Mehoffer, Weiss and a sculptor, Dunikowski. Most of them taught at the Academy of Fine Arts and exerted considerable influence on the young

generation of painters. On the other hand however, there appeared a growing tendency to break away from the tradition and catch up with the European avant-garde. Young artists formed groups assuming often very radical programs. An example of such a group were the Formists, active already since 1917, and among them Tytus Czyżewski, Zbigniew and Andrzej Pronaszko, Tymon Niesiołowski, August Zamoyski, Leon Chwistek and Stanisław Ignacy Witkiewicz. The latter two were not only active painters but also the theoreticians of the group. Formism drew on the legacies of Cubism, Expressionism and Futurism, putting basic stress on formal coherence of a piece of art. A few new initiatives appeared in the period between the wars. In 1923 a group of students of the Academy started the so-called Paris Committee with the intention of pursuing studies in France. Members of the Committee were Jan Cybis, Hanna Rudzka-Cybisowa, Józef Czapski, Zygmunt Waliszewski, Artur Nacht-Samborski, Józef Jarema and Tadeusz Piotr Potworowski. In 1925 the members of the Committee went to France, where they stayed until 1931. The aforementioned artists were mainly the representatives of Colourism which dominated Polish art in the thirties and in the period immediately following the Second World War. In 1925 the "Jednoróg" (The Unicorn), Arts Guild was formed, with Jan Rubczak, Felicjan Szczęsny Kowarski and Jerzy Fedkowicz. In 1928 another group, the "Zwornik" (The Keystone) became active, its leading members being Emil Krcha and Czesław Rzepiński. Maria Jarema, Henryk Wiciński and Jonasz Stern were main representatives of a radically avant-garde and leftist oriented group known as "The Cracow Group" which was formed in 1933.

Despite the avant-garde groups being in opposition to the artistic traditions, some of their members were granted prestigious state commissions which is an evidence of openness of the artistic circles. Felicjan Kowarski, Leonard Pękalski, Józef Jarema, and the much older Józef Pankiewicz were asked to make the plafond paintings in Wawel Castle. The representatives of the avant-garde trends of the period between the wars generally did not win the popularity comparable to that enjoyed by the artists of Young Poland. Their works are more complex in perception and more distant from the traditional ideas of understanding art. Still, the talents and deep theoretical knowledge were of profound importance for the survival of the independent spirit of Polish art during the years of the Nazi occupation and later in the period of socrealistic dictatorship.

Based in Cracow was also the literary avant-garde movement grouped around Tadeusz Peiper and the journals "Zwrotnica" and "Linia" (among others - Julian Przyboś and Jalu Kurek). The meeting point of writers and representatives of visual arts

In September 1939 Cracow, unlike Warsaw, was not defended by the Polish Army and on the sixth day of the war German troops entered the city. Already in October it became the capital city of the so-called General Government, covering a large part of Poland. Cracow was divided into sectors. The modern western districts were reserved for the Germans and their Polish residents were forced to move to Stradom and Kazimierz. A Jewish ghetto was created in Podgórze. Higher and secondary schools were closed. The repressions struck all social groups and in particular the intelligentsia. On November 6th 1939 the Nazi arrested 184 professors of the Cracow institutions of higher education and deported them to the Sachsenhausen concentration camp. On April 19th 1942, two hundred artists were sent to Auschwitz. The most tragic was the fate of the Jewish community in Cracow numbering around 55 thousand before the war. The inhuman living conditions and executions in the Plaszów and Auschwitz camps resulted in only a thousand of them to surviving. The picture of their ordeal, brightened up with the light of human solidarity became well known in the world thanks to the book and film "Schindler's List".

The occupants treated Cracow as their permanent possession and did everything to impose a German character on the city. Wawel Castle became the seat of the German authorities with the Governor Hans Frank. Polish monuments were destroyed, including, the monuments in memory of the Battle of Grunwald, Mickiewicz and Kościuszko. An organised robbery of cultural goods was carried out and some of them are still missing. The greatest loss is Raphael Santi's "Portrait of a Young Man" from the Czartoryski Museum.

The German terror was obviously opposed by the Poles, hence the majority of the most valuable national treasures were either hidden or taken out of the city. Polish underground organisations of various political ideologies became active from the very beginning of the occupation. Cracow, after Warsaw, was the second centre of active resistance of Armia Krajowa (The Home Army). Secret education at all levels was soon started. There were even underground theatrical performances in which Karol Wojtyła (later Pope John Paul II) and Tadeusz Kantor made their first steps towards fame. The war fate of Cracow was far less severe than in Warsaw. The occupation ended after five years and five months, on 18th January 1945. The Second Ukrainian Front troops managed to force the Germans out of the city due to a successful surrounding manoeuvre. The Nazis fled before they had time to detonate the explosives planted under the major buildings of the city. Once again Cracow avoided major fights and destruction except for the demolised bridges and minor damage to the Cathedral.

was the Cricot Theatre.

The post-war period, still the present day for the majority of the Cracovians, has fast grown to last for half of a century, bringing enormous changes in the conditions of everyday life of the city. Immediately after the end of the war it was easy to hope that the end of the German occupation would mean a return to the pre-war relations. It soon turned out; however, that the new laws in Poland were enforced in such a way that they had little in common with freedom and democracy. Cracow attempted resistance. In 1946 the vote in the Cracow referendum which intended to authorise a change in the system was blankly opposed and it was impossible to falsify the result or hide it from the public. The city earned the status of the "centre of reaction" which had to bring serious consequences in the future.

At first, few changes could be observed in the everyday life. There was little damage. Trade and small business were quickly restored. Already in spring 1945 the University and other institutions of higher education began to function. An entirely new problem was that of overpopulation. The undamaged city attracted thousands of people whom the war had forced to leave their former homes. Despite the loss of almost all the Jewish inhabitants, already in 1945 the population of Cracow reached 300 thousand. With time, the rapid growth of population became the result of the social engineering methods used by the communist authorities, as a means to change the oppositional nature of the city. The major project undertaken as a result was the construction of a gigantic steelworks around which the "socialist" town of Nowa Huta was built, now one of the biggest quarters of Cracow.

In 1963 the population reached 518 thousand and in 1980 - around 700 thousand. This growing number of people needed flats to live in. Primarily, the whole effort was centred on building Nowa Huta, and with time, numerous other districts, or rather huge clusters of blocks of flats began to appear. It was the quantity and not the quality that mattered and urban planning was non-existent. The historical panorama of the city, still present in the post-war period, was lost beyond the point of return.

Such negative phenomena obviously do not convey the entire picture of life in Cracow under the communist rule. Thousands of people coming from villages upgraded their standard of life, the education system was developed, culture grew amidst relatively good conditions. Nevertheless the price for these gains, belonging to the general trend of progress of civilisation in the post-war world, was too high, and erroneous decisions led to consequences which hang and will hang heavily over the city for decades to come.

For the whole post-war period, Cracow shared the fate of the whole country. If there was anything specific to Cracow, it

was the love of tradition and quiet, wise endurance, reluctant to all forms of radicalism.

The culture of Cracow over the 50 year post-war period presents a colourful and diverse picture. Influenced to a certain degree by political events whilst simultaneously being independent from them or sometimes even shaped just to spite the existence supposed to define awareness. Since the early post-war years Cracow has regained and even strengthened its role as a cultural centre, attracting a number of homeless authors. The intellectual circles were not crushed in the years of the Stalinist suppression though they suffered heavy blows. These included the liquidation of the Polish Academy of Arts and Sciences in 1952, the closing of the Theological Faculty of the University and other disintegrating moves. The University, amongst other institutions of higher education managed to maintain their high standards and stayed faithful to the academic values both during the March 1968 students' unrest and throughout the Marshal Law period. Consequently since 1989 they have become the source of highly qualified professionals. Among writers, permanently or temporarily linked to Cracow we should mention Konstanty Ildefons Gałczyński, Tadeusz Breza, Jalu Kurek, Julian Przyboś, Antoni Gołubiew, Karol Bunsch, Stanisław Lem, Sławomir Mrożek, Jan Józef Szczepański, Wisława Szymborska and Jerzy Harasymowicz. In recent years Czesław Miłosz has also chosen to reside in Cracow for several months during the year.

As regards the fine arts those active in the early post-war years were the last representatives of the Young Poland. First of all Józef Mehoffer, Wojciech Weiss, Karol Frycz and Xawery Dunikowski who provided a specific continuation to the Cracow's tradition. Others included an active group of artists who made their names in the interwar period - Eugeniusz Eibisch, Zbigniew Pronaszko, Hanna Rudzka-Cybisowa, Jerzy Fedkowicz, Czesław Rzepiński and Wacław Taranczewski. Many of them headed departments in the Academy of Fine Arts and exerted influence on the younger generations. Of greatest importance among the painters who started their careers in the initial post-war were the Group of Young Artists which in 1957 took over the name of the pre-war Cracow Group. Its members were, among others, Tadeusz Brzozowski, Andrzej Wróblewski, Jerzy Nowosielski, Jerzy Tchórzewski, Kazimierz Mikulski and Tadeusz Kantor who apart from his painting experiments, won world-wide fame as the author of the "Cricot 2" theatrical performances.

The sculpture in Cracow can be divided into two distinctive trends: the academic trend connected with the monumental works (Dunikowski, Konieczny) and the avant-garde, experimenting with the material and stylistic structures of works of art (Bronisław Chromy, Marian Kruczek, Jerzy Bereś).

Though much, perhaps even too much has been built in Cracow in the last fifty years, there are no structures that could match the historical tradition of the city. The "old" centre of Nowa Huta designed according to the conventional axis type urban planning practice was built in the banal forms of simplified socrealism. The large construction boom of the sixties and the seventies was dominated by a tendency to save on finances and materials, which resulted in popular use of large slab technology, destroying all individual approach. Under the circumstances, the only ambitious projects appeared in the religious architecture. They are the two churches, The Church of Our Lady the Queen of Poland in Bieńczyce (Wojciek Pietrzyk, 1967) and the Church of St. Maximilian Kolbe in Mistrzejowice (Józef Dutkiewicz, 1976). Postmodernism, germinating in the eighties, has not taken flight contrary to what was hoped for. Cracow is still awaiting the architectural breakthrough worth the coming 21st century. A breakthrough which would turn it into a truly modern city without impairing its old historical structure.

The greatest achievements of the Cracow theatre, except for the already mentioned avant-garde "Cricot 2", have been the performances directed by Konrad Swinarski, Andrzej Wajda and Jerzy Jarocki in the Stary Theatre. Special attention should be given to the "Piwnica pod Baranami" cabaret , proud of its 40-year tradition and of the unique atmosphere created by late Piotr Skrzynecki. Music in Cracow is mainly represented by the world famous composer Krzysztof Penderecki, but well worth mentioning is the excellent Philharmonic Orchestra and numerous performers of old music of which the Capella Cracoviensis, directed by Stanisław Gałoński, deserves a special mention.

Our short summary is unable to present a comprehensive review of the thousand-year-old history of the city and its culture. Its objective is to provide some information and comments to the vision contained in the photographs of Adam Bujak and to encourage individual encounters with Cracow. Those who wish to extend this knowledge have numerous sources at their disposal, from guide books and synthetic outlines to specialist academic periodicals. It is sometimes worth making use of this abundance of information. Reading about Cracow is a necessity if you truly want to read Cracow.

Jan K. Ostrowski

The Royal City of Cracow with the Vistula River. A bird-eye view.

Outside the City Walls

The Premonstratensian Convent in the district of Zwierzyniec is one of the most beautiful architectural complexes in Cracow, outside the Old Town.

44 Outside the City Walls   The Benedictine Monastery in Tyniec near Cracow. Benedictines came here
in the second half of the 11th century, invited by Boleslaus the Bold.

The wooden church in the district of Mogiła, not far from the Cistercian Monastery.

The famous miracle-working crucifix in the Cistercian Monastery in the district of Mogiła.

48 Outside the City Walls

The Church of the Holiest Saviour in the district of Salwator. One of the oldest churches in Cracow. According to a legend it was consecrated by St. Adalbert.

St. Margaret's wooden church in the district of Salwator is octagonal in shape. It was built after the fire of 1690 on the spot of the former church.

50 Outside the City Walls   The church in Arena, dedicated to the Visitation of the Holy Virgin Mary
and the Carmelite Monastery were erected for Ladislaus Jagiełło and Jadwiga.

The cover of the medieval code, which is kept in the Carmelite Monastery in Arena.

The Carmelite Monastery in Arena possesses some exceptionally precious medieval codes with magnificent, colourful miniatures.

A fragment of the altar in the church of St. Bernardino of Siena. The monumental sculptures in the altar were made, among others, by Antoni Gegenpauer.

The altar of the Madonna and Child in the Church of Friars Observant in the district of Stradom, in the part of the church designed for the friars.

56 Outside the City Walls

The oldest fragments of St. Nicholas' Church go back to the 13th century.
The Benedictines of Tyniec bequeathed that church to the University.

The 18th century façade of the church of the Carmelite nuns in Kopernika Street.

The banisters in the House of Physicians were designed in 1905 by Stanisław Wyspiański.

A stained-glass window by Stanisław Wyspiański in the House of Physicians.

A panorama of Cracow with the focus on the cemetery in the district of Rakowice on All Saints' Day.

62 Outside the City Walls

The gable of the "Spider House" in Karmelicka Street was designed by Teodor Talowski, the author of a number of buildings in Cracow.

The finial of the former Pusłowski Palace. At present it houses the Department of Musicology of the Jagiellonian University.

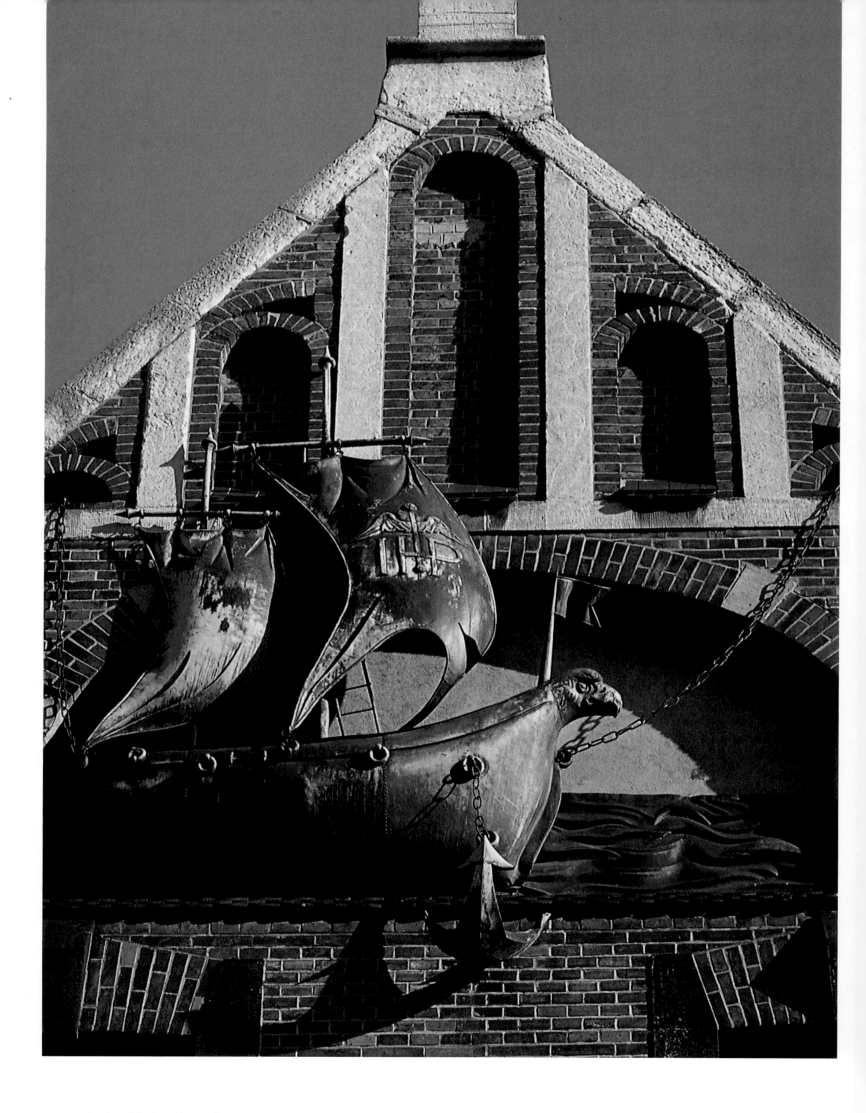

64 Outside the City Walls

The "Globe House", the former headquarters of the Chamber of Commerce and Industry, built according to the design by T. Stryjeński and F. Mączyński.

The façade of the Provincial House belonging to the Convent of the Daughters of God's Mercy. Today it houses a dormitory for girls.

66 Outside the City Walls

St. Florian's Church founded by Casimir the Just in the 12th century.
Karol Wojtyła – the present Pope, John Paul II – was its curate in the years 1949-51.

St. Florian's Church, dating from the early Middle Ages. The present interior decoration goes back mostly to the 17th and 18th centuries.

68 Outside the City Walls

The Matejko Square with the Grunwald Monument founded in 1910 by Ignacy Paderewski to commemorate the 500th anniversary of the battle of Grunwald.

70 Outside the City Walls

The building of the Academy of Fine Arts named after Jan Matejko, an eminent painter who was one of the rectors of the Academy.

The machiculation with loop-holes in the upper part of the Barbican,
which is the largest preserved defensive structure of that kind in Europe.

St. Florian's Gate was built in the 13th century, but the brick superstructure with the stone machiculation was added as late as the 15th century.

St. Florian's Gate, the Baribican and the Haberdashers' and Carpenters' Towers are the only preserved fragments of the medieval city walls.

The Old Town

After the charter of 1257 the Market Square became the new city center. The irregular shape of Grodzka Street testifies to the pre-charter arrangement of buildings.

The Old Town 75

The auditorium in the theatre named after Juliusz Słowacki. It is impressive in size. There are as many as 922 seats.

The foyer in the theatre named after J. Słowacki. The solemn inauguration of the theatre took place in 1893.

The theatre named after J. Słowacki was built at the end of the 19th century according to the design by Jan Zawieyski. It was modelled on the Grand Opera in Paris.

The pond with the fountain was created in 1904. It was to improve the microclimate of the Planty Gardens, which continuously suffered from lack of water.

The interior of the small Holy Cross Church. The chancel came into being about the year 1300, while the nave goes back to the middle of the 14th century.

The chancel of the Holy Cross Church with its richly decorated Baroque altar.

The Old Town 83

The complex of buildings around the viridarium of the Franciscan Monastery was finished before 1455. The gothic murals go back to the period of its erection.

A stained-glass window with the scene of St. Francis' ecstasy, made according to the design by Stanisław Wyspiański.

The banisters at the Franciscan Monastery visible from the Plac Wszystkich Świętych (All Saints' Square).

The Old Town 87

The Lady with the Ermine, a picture by Leonardo da Vinci, from the precious art collection, brought to Cracow by Duke Władysław Czartoryski.

The Czartoryski Museum. The exhibition is arranged in the Arsenal converted into a museum by Duke Władysław Czartoryski.

The domes of the chapels of the Dominican Church.

The picture of Our Lady of the Rosary in one of the chapels of the Dominican
Church. After the victory of Vienna King John III Sobieski had the chapel expanded.

The Old Town 91

The reliquaries and monstrances in the treasury at the Dominican Monastery.
Although the Dominicans were a mendicant order, they always had rich donors.

Nowodworski's College erected in the 17th century, designed by Jan Leitner.
At present it houses the Faculty of Medicine of the Jagiellonian University.

The alchemical laboratory in the Jagiellonian University Museum in the Collegium Maius.

The Old Town 95

Two buildings destroyed by two fires were reconstructed and merged into one at the end of the 15th century. Such were the origins of the Collegium Maius.

The cloisters in the Collegium Maius, the oldest preserved building of the Jagiellonian University, built thanks to the legacy of Queen Jadwiga.

A gilded globe dating back to 1510 with a clock mechanism and a calendar
– a possession of the Jagiellonian University Museum in the Collegium Maius.

The University Museum. The globes, astrolabes and other instruments for the observation and measurement of the positions of stars.

The Dominican Convent in the district of Gródek, erected in the 17th century on the spot of a manor-house of Mayor Albert and of a tiny castle of Ladislaus the Short.

The Planty Gardens next to the outer wall of St. Peter and St. Paul's Church.
Numerous monasteries in Cracow were located next to the city walls.

Cracow developed around Wawel Hill. From its top one can see as far as the most distant borders of the city.

The architectural shape of the 17th-century Jesuit Church of St. Peter and St. Paul, was created by a number of artists. Its founder, priest Piotr Skarga, is buried in its vaults.

The Old Town 105

St. Andrew's Church was built after 1260, on the old foundations
of the 11th century church that had been probably destroyed by the Tartars.

The reliquaries made in Mainz early in the 13th century are kept by Poor Clares, the oldest convent in Cracow situated at St. Andrew's Church.

The Old Town 107

The Baroque statues of the twelve Apostles in front of St. Peter and St. Paul's Church. St. Andrew's Romanesque church is visible in the background.

The Św. Marii Magdaleny Square, formerly the Veit Stoss' Square. It was the center of the Okół, a settlement area developing at the foot of Wawel Hill.

St. Giles' Church was built in the 14th century. At present it is also used by the Armenian denomination. The Katyń memorial cross stands in front of the church.

The façade of St. Martin's Church, which nowadays belongs to the Augsburg Protestant congregation in Cracow.

The stairs at the entrance to the Baroque 18th-century Piarist Church dedicated to the Transfiguration is the work of Kasper Bażanka.

The University Baroque Church of St. Anne's was erected in the years 1689-1705, on the site of the former church designed by Tylman of Gameren.

The finial of the high altar in St. Anne's Church – the sculptures by Baltazar Fontana date from the end of the 17th century.

The Old Town 115

In 1655 the Reformati took refuge from the Swedes within the city walls.
The microclimate in the monastery vaults helped to preserve the bodies of the dead.

The monument of Józef Dietl in front of the building of the Municipal Council. The statue was sculpted by Xawery Dunikowski in 1938.

The courtyard of the Collegium Iuridicum. From the beginning of the 15th century the building housed the Faculty of Law of the Cracow Academy.

The Planty Gardens – a picturesque park surrounding the Old Town. It was established at the beginning of the 19th century, on the site of the medieval city walls.

The monument of Lilla Weneda by Alfred Daun. It was founded in 1884 by Henryk
Jordan to commemorate the 35th anniversary of Słowacki's death.

The Old Town 121

The Archeological Museum in the buildings of the former St. Michael's Church and the Monastery of Discalced Carmelites.

A bird-eye view of Cracow. The prominent buildings are: the Franciscan and
Dominican monasteries and the huge building of the Main Post Office.

The Old Town 123

The church of Our Lady of the Snow and the Dominican Convent founded by
Anna Lubomirska, née Branicka, as a votive offering for the victory of Chocim.

The Market Square

A view of the Market Square from the dome of St. Anne's Church. The mascarons on the Renaissance attic of the Cloth Hall are probably the work of Santi Gucci.

The contest of Cracovian cribs near Mickiewicz's monument in the Main Market Square takes place every year, on the first Thursday of the Advent.

The authors of the cribs are inspired by the elements of the old architecture of Cracow.

130 The Market Square

The City Hall Tower in the Main Market Square is the remnant of the Cracow's city hall, built at the turn of the 13th century.

The city hall was pulled down at the beginning of the 19th century. In the past its vaults housed the city dungeon. Today there is a cafe and a theatre.

The Cloth Hall. The rooms on the first floor house the Gallery of Polish Painting, which is a branch of the National Museum.

134 The Market Square

The Cloth Hall, erected during the reign of Casimir the Great, in the 14th century. After the fire of 1555 its reconstruction was supervised by Giovanni Padovano.

The Cloth Hall has preserved its commercial function. It houses a number of souvenir stalls.

136 The Market Square

A procession of Cracovians with a traditional loaf of bread made for the Harvest Festival.

During each of the visits to Poland, Pope John Paul II finds some time to meet the Cracovians. For a number of years he was their Archbishop.

138 The Market Square

The Hobby-Horse – „Lajkonik". Every year, on the last of the eight days of Corpus Christi celebrations, its picturesque pageant heads for the Main Market Square.

A traditional Cracovian wedding pageant with horse-drawn carriages.

140 The Market Square   St. Mary's Church, dedicated to the Assumption of the Holy Virgin Mary.
The Gothic brick church was erected in the last years of the 13th century.

The altar by Veit Stoss after close. The relief sculptures present the scenes from Mary's life and the Passion.

The late-Gothic high altar at St. Mary's was carved by Veit Stoss and his pupils in the years 1477-89.

144 The Market Square   Virgin Mary in the temple. One of the scenes from the inner side of the altar wing at St. Mary's Church.

Expressive faces of the apostles supporting Mary – the central part of the altar with the scene of Mary's falling asleep.

146 The Market Square

The crucifix in one of the aisles at St. Mary's. It was sculpted at the end of the 15th century by Veit Stoss.

The feet of crucified Christ – a fragment of the sculpture by Veit Stoss at St. Mary's.

A bird-eye view of Cracow with the prominent silhouette of St. Mary's Church.

The District of Kazimierz

The Town Hall of Kazimierz, the town founded in the 14th century by King Casimir the Great. At present the building houses the Ethnographic Museum.

The District of Kazimierz 151

A fragment of the railing around the pool going back to 1723, in the courtyard of the Paulite Monastery on Skałka.

The statue of St. Stanislaus and the gate leading to the pool, on the site of the Bishop's martyrdom in the 11th century.

The District of Kazimierz 153

The church dedicated to Michael the Archangel and St. Stanislaus the Bishop on Skałka. The Baroque basilica was built in the first half of the 18th century.

The neighbourhood of the Paulite Monastery on Skałka. St. Catherine's Gothic church is visible in the background.

The celebrations dedicated to St. Stanislaus on Skałka. The crypt of the Paulite church is a necropolis of many famous Poles.

The choir gallery and the organ, suspended over the stalls in the Corpus Christi Church, go back to the third quarter of the 17th century.

The interior of the 14th-century Corpus Christi Church. According to a legend it was built on the spot where a stolen monstrance had been miraculously recovered.

The boat-shaped pulpit, dating back to the middle of the 18th century, in the Gothic Corpus Christi Church.

The interior of the 14th-century Corpus Christi Church. According to a legend it was built on the spot where a stolen monstrance had been miraculously recovered.

The boat-shaped pulpit, dating back to the middle of the 18th century, in the Gothic Corpus Christi Church.

One of the mermaids that support the boat-shaped pulpit in the Corpus Christi Church.

St. Catherine's Church was erected in the 60s and 70s of the 14th century for the Augustinians who came from Prague, invited by King Casimir the Great.

The high altar in the Gothic St. Catherine's Church goes back to 1634. The picture, St. Catherine's Mystic Wedding, was painted by Andrzej Wenest in 1674.

The neo-Gothic stalls in St. Catherine's Church. This church of exceptional beauty was saved from demolition that was planned in the 19th century.

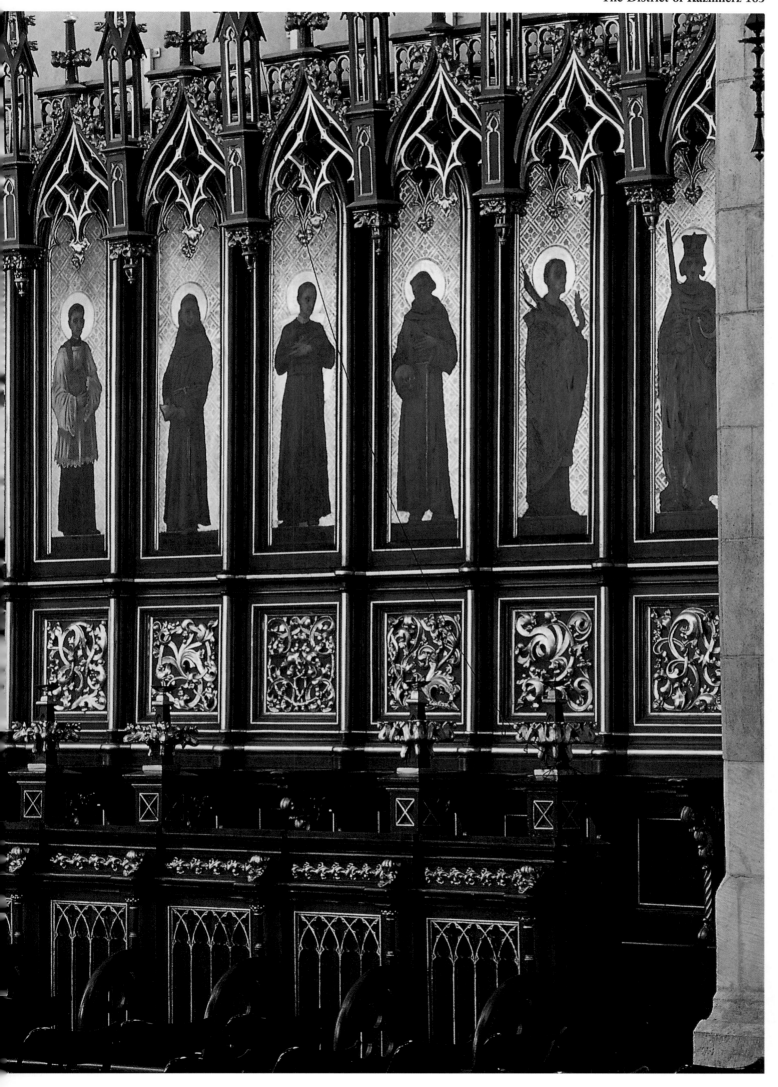

At the end of April or at the beginning of May, the Jews from all over the world meet at the Remuh Synagogue to celebrate the death anniversary of Rabbi Moses Isserles.

A solemn concert in the Tempel Synagogue in the district of Kazimierz, during the
Jewish Culture Festival.

The District of Kazimierz 167

The interior of the Remuh Synagogue. It was founded by Rabbi Remuh's father, Israel Isserles, who came from Regensburg in the middle of the 16th century.

The bimah inside the Renaissance building of the Old Synagogue. The exhibition dedicated to the history of the Jews is a branch of the Historical Museum.

Szeroka Street in the district of Kazimierz with the building of the Old Synagogue. The final concerts of the Jewish Culture Festival take place here.

The Jewish cemetery in Miodowa Street. It is still the burial place of the Jewish community.

The view of the former Town of Kazimierz from Wawel Hill with the prominent silhouettes of two mighty Gothic churches – Corpus Christi and St. Catherine's.

The Royal Castle

The Hen's Foot Tower and the Gothic Annexe – fragments of the late medieval Royal Castle on the north-eastern side of Wawel Hill.

The complex of the buildings on Wawel Hill is irregular in shape. The attic finishing the southern wing of the castle.

The building of the gate leading to the courtyard of the Royal Castle. The portal was
decorated by Bartolomeo Berrecci in the 20s and 30s of the 16th century.

The procession of the kings heading for Wawel Castle. Wacław Szymanowski's design of a monument can be seen at the National Museum in Cracow.

The columns of the gallery on the second floor of Wawel Castle.

The courtyard of Wawel Castle was built at the end of the 15th century. The construction was supervised by Francis of Florence, Master Benedict and B. Berrecci.

The galleries on the second floor of the northern wing. The tall, slim columns are additionally strengthened in the middle.

The room inside the Hen's Foot Tower came into being at the beginning of the 17th century. King Sigismund III Vasa had his alchemical laboratory nearby.

The Royal Castle 187

The Hall of Senators on the second floor of the Royal Castle.

The royal throne in the Hall of Senators. The tapestry on the wall, belongs to the collection made in Brussels and commissioned by King Sigismund Augustus.

A coat of arms of the Crown – a fragment of a Wawel tapestry.
One of the tapestries made in the workshops in Brussels, in the years 1552-71.

The Royal Castle 191

The so-called Planet Hall on the second floor of the eastern wing of the Royal Castle. The tapestry on the wall presents a unicorn-giraffe.

The so-called Zodiac Hall with the frieze composed of the signs of the Zodiac.
The tapestry on the wall, with Noah meeting God, belongs to the Noah series.

Noah with his wife before boarding the Ark. A fragment of one of the Wawel tapestries from the Noah series.

A fragment of the tapestry illustrating the Deluge. It is one of the Noah series.

The Royal Castle 195

The vestibule between the Hall of Senators and the Eagle Hall, called the Pallas
Athena Room. The equestrian portrait of Ladislaus IV was painted by P.P. Rubens.

A motif from the tapestry with a unicorn-giraffe, belonging to the animal series. They were probably made according to the cartoons by Wilhelm Tons.

Under his death will King Sigismund Augustus bequeathed the tapestries to the Polish State.

The Royal Castle 199

The Bird Hall in the north-eastern part of the castle. The wallpaper is made of cordovan in régence style.

The castle chapel on the second floor of the Royal Castle, next to the Head Hall.

The Royal Castle 201

The ceiling of the Hall of Envoys, also known as the Head Hall. All heads in the coffers were sculpted in the first half of the 16th century.

One of the heads on the ceiling in the Head Hall. At present there are only 30 heads, but in the past there was a head in each of the coffers.

The Royal Castle 203

The Hall of Envoys. According to a legend one of the heads addressed the King during a trial he presided over: „King Augustus pass a just judgement."

Rapiers used in various European countries from the 16th to the 18th century.

The Royal Castle 207

„Wawel that is no more." The interior of the pre-Romanesque church – the Virgin Mary's Rotunda – dating from the turn of the 10th century.

„Wawel that is no more." A stone column in St. Gereon's Church, whose construction was begun in 1020 in the times of King Boleslaus the Brave.

The Royal Castle 209

The discovered foundations of the first Cathedral, which was partly pulled down as early as the second half of the 11th century.

The travelling chalice, calix viaticus, and the paten found in an abbot's tomb in Tyniec near Cracow. They were made in the 11th century, probably in Cracow.

The southern elevation of the castle courtyard with the frieze under the ceiling of the second floor gallery.

„Szczerbiec"– the jagged sword. According to a legend it was jagged when Boleslaus the Bold struck the gates of Kiev, but in fact it goes back to the 13th century.

„Szczerbiec" in the Crown Treasury. Since 1320, the year of Ladislaus the Short's coronation, it was the coronation sword of the Polish kings.

The Royal Castle 215

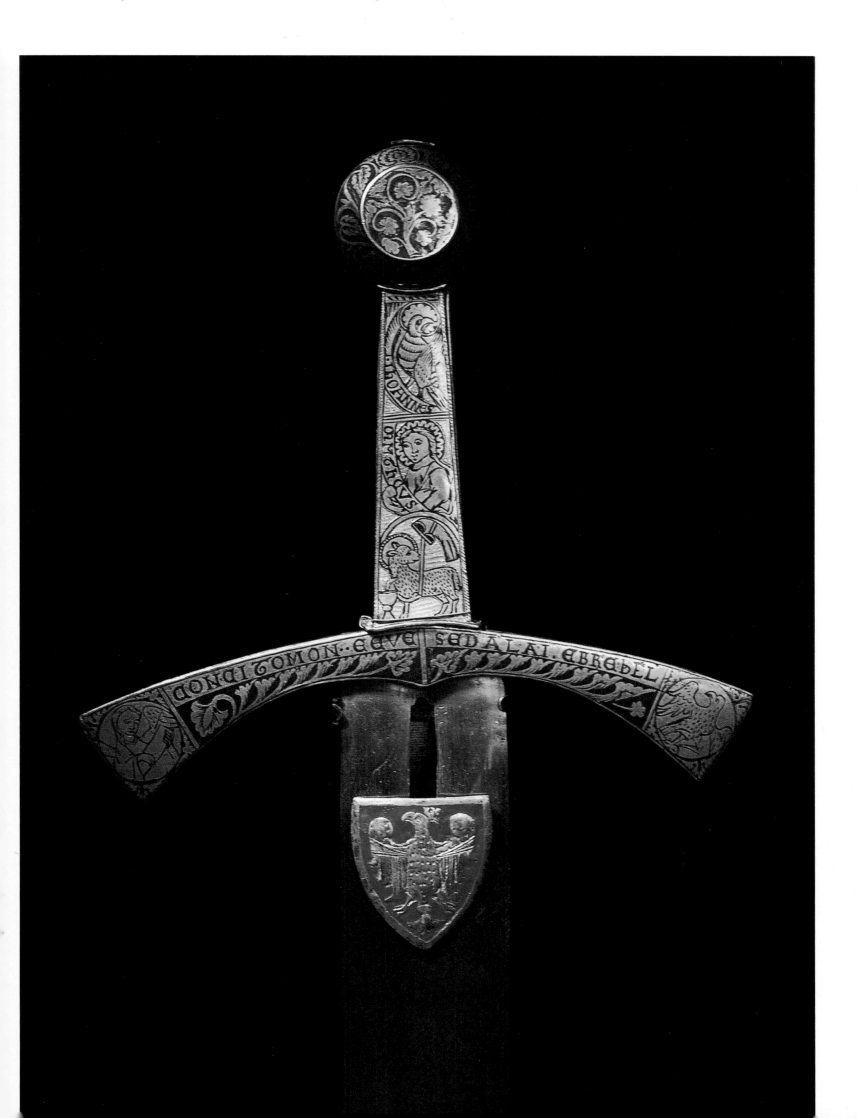

Wawel Armoury with the exhibition of shaft-mounted weapons and the replicas of the banners taken from the Teutonic Knights in the battle of Grunwald in 1410.

A part of the exhibition „Wawel that is no more" with the models of the former buildings.

The Royal Castle 217

The Armoury. The back of the tournament armour made in Nuremberg in 1496, in Konrad Poler's workshop.

An 18th-century Polish hussar's suit of armour with a characteristic pair of wings and a hauberk.

The Treasury. The goblets from the collection of the Radziwiłł family of Nieśwież; made in Germany at the end of the 16th century.

222 The Royal Castle

The Armoury. The chain armour of Ladislaus IV made in Transylvania in the first half of the 17th century.

The pommel of the sword made in Germany in the 16th century. The sword was
a gift from Ladislaus Sigismund for Piotr Konaszewicz Sahajdaczy.

The Royal Castle 223

Fighting knights – a fragment of the frieze in the Tournament Hall. The frieze was partly painted by Hans Dürer.

The Treasury. A cup with Jan Opaliński's crest and with the effigy of King Stanisław Leszczyński's. It was made in 1712, probably in Gdańsk.

The Royal Castle 225

The Sandomierska Tower going back to the second half of the 15th century and the so-called Bernardyńska Gate on the south-eastern side of Wawel Hill.

Wawel Hill as seen from the right bank of the Vistula River.

The Cathedral

The magnificent edifice of Wawel Cathedral as seen from the Planty Gardens.

232 The Cathedral

A tusk of a mammoth and bones of other diluvial animals suspended next to the main entrance to Wawel Cathedral.

The door to Wawel Cathedral, dating from the second half of the 14th century, with the multiplied Casimir the Great's monogram – the crowned letter K.

234 The Cathedral The main entrance to the Cathedral with the Holy Trinity Chapel on the right, and the Holy Cross Chapel, on the left.

The domes of Bishop Jakub Zadzik's Chapel, the Sigismund Chapel and the Vasa Chapel on the southern side of the Cathedral.

236 The Cathedral   The southern side of the Cathedral with the sepulchral chapels of kings and bishops.

The scale-like pattern on the gold dome of the Sigismund Chapel.

The chancel of Wawel Cathedral during the annual service for the dead.

242 The Cathedral

The nave of Wawel Cathedral, dedicated to St. Wenceslas and St. Stanislaus the Bishop. The nave and the two aisles of the church were completed in 1364.

The silver coffin of St. Stanislaus the Bishop. It was made in the years 1670-71 in Gdańsk, financed from the legacy bequeathed by Bishop Piotr Gembicki.

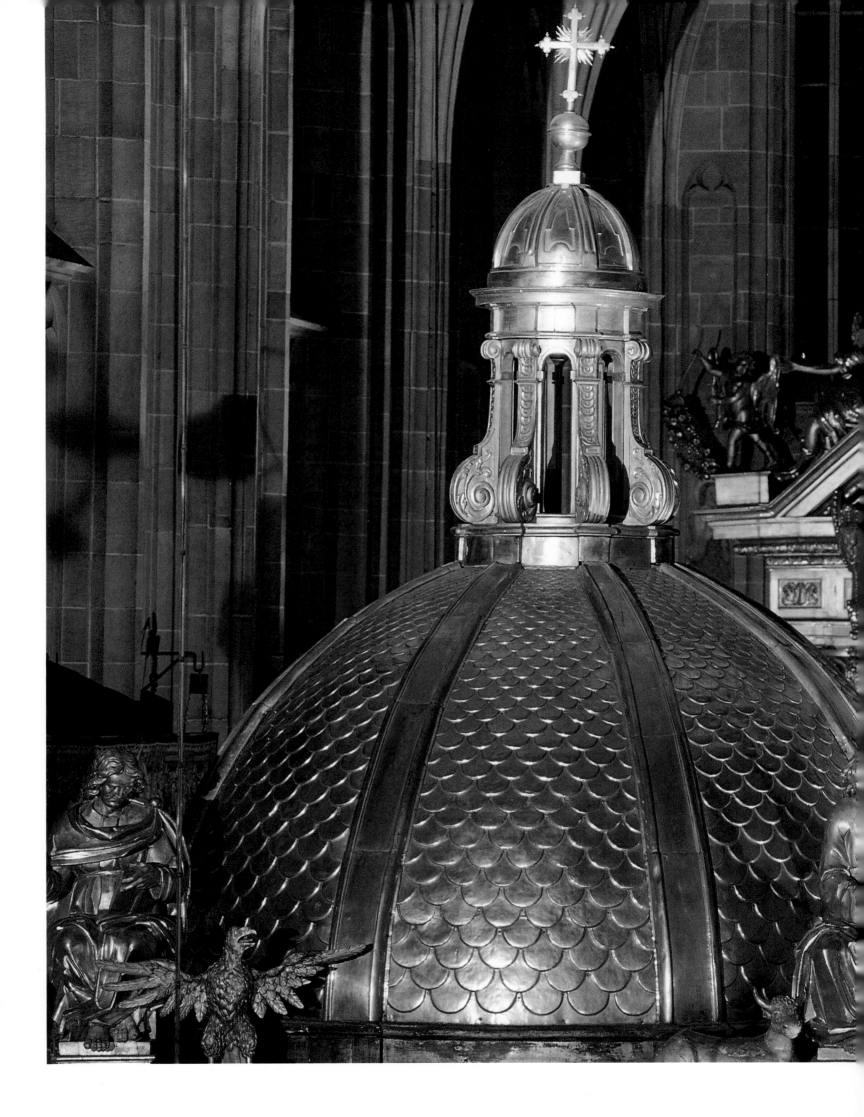

The dome of St. Stanislaus' mausoleum, founded by Bishop Szyszkowski in the 20s of the 17th century, designed by Giovanni Trevano.

246 The Cathedral   The vault above the choir gallery.

The shrine of the martyr – St. Stanislaus the Bishop.

The bishop's throne in the chancel of Wawel Cathedral, which is dedicated to St. Wenceslas and St. Stanislaus the Bishop.

During the first visit to Poland, in June 1979, Pope John Paul II visited Wawel Cathedral.

250 The Cathedral During the pilgrimage to his homeland in 1997 the Pope prayed in Wawel Cathedral in front of the Black Crucifix also known as Queen Jadwiga's Crucifix.

Queen Jadwiga's Black Crucifix in Wawel Cathedral, in the north-eastern part of the ambulatory. The sculpture of Christ goes back to the 14th century.

The sarcophagus of St. Jadwiga the Queen in the southern ambulatory, sculpted in Carrara marble by Antoni Madeyski, in Rome, in 1902.

The sarcophagus of King Casimir the Great. The canopy was probably paid for and ordered to place by Casimir's sister, Elizabeth, Queen of Hungary.

The head of the King – a fragment of the sculpture on Casimir the Great's sarcophagus.

The sarcophagus of King Casimir Jagiellon in the Holy Cross Chapel in Wawel
Cathedral. It is the work of Veit Stoss and Jorge Hubert and it geos back to 1492.

King Casimir Jagiellon's head. A fragment of the marble sculpture by Veit Stoss from the sarcophagus of the King.

258 The Cathedral

One of the sculpted images of mourners from the marble sarcophagus of King Casimir Jagiellon.

The decorative element of one of the columns supporting the canopy of Casimir Jagiellon's sarcophagus.

The head of King Ladislaus Jagiełło. A fragment of the sarcophagus going back to the first half of the 15th century.

The sarcophagus of King Ladislaus Jagiełło. The Renaissance canopy made by Giovanni Cini of Siena was probably designed by Bartolomeo Berrecci.

The head of King Ladislaus the Short. The sarcophagus in the northern arm of the
ambulatory dates from the first half of the 14th century.

264 The Cathedral The interior of the 16th-century dome of the Sigismund Chapel.
Designed by Bartolomeo Berrecci, it is a masterpiece of Polish Renaissance.

The sepulchral wall in the Sigismund Chapel in Wawel Cathedral, with the sculpted images of two kings – Sigismund the Old and Sigismund Augustus.

The sepulchre of Queen Anne Jagiellon in the Sigismund Chapel. It was sculpted by Santi Gucci in the years 1574-75.

Queen Anne Jagiellon's head on her sepulcher in the Sigismund Chapel in Wawel Cathedral.

Sigismund the Old – the sepulchral sculpture going back to the years 1521-1531.
It was probably carved by Bartolomeo Berrecci.

The dome of the Vasa Chapel inside. The chapel dates from the second half of the 17th century.

An ornamental element from the dome of the Vasa Chapel.

One of the stained-glass windows designed by Józef Mehoffer in 1909.

A symbolical sarcophagus of King Ladislaus III Warneńczyk, who lost his life
fighting with the Turks in the battle of Varna.

All Souls' Day decorations in Wawel Cathedral. The statue of the Resurrected Christ with the symbols of the royal and episcopal power.

The Holy Saturday celebrations in Wawel Cathedral.

All Souls' Day in Wawel Cathedral. Every year the clergy of Cracow take part
in the service dedicated to the kings, bishops and national heroes entombed here.

The lamp in the shape of a stylized crown in the Jagiellon crypt.

The manneristic tin sarcophagi of Sigismund Augustus and Anne Jagiellon made in Gdańsk in the second half of the 16th century.

The copper sarcophagus of Queen Cecilia Renata, Ladislaus IV's wife, with wrought and gilded ornaments.

King Ladislaus IV's copper sarcophagus with gilded elements. Next to it the coffin of his son, Sigismund Casimir.

King John Casimir's sarcophagus made of sandstone in the second half of the 17th century, paid for and ordered to place by King John III Sobieski.

The Crypt of Marshal Józef Piłsudski under the Tower of the Silver Bells.

The Romanesque Crypt of St. Leonard. The last resting-place of King John III Sobieski, Duke Józef Poniatowski and Tadeusz Kościuszko.

The beatification ceremony of Queen Jadwiga held by Pope John Paul II in 1987.

The epitaph plate of Bishop Marcin Szyszkowski in the wall of the nave, near St. Stanislaus' shrine.

288 The Cathedral

St. Mary's Chapel in the eastern part of Wawel Cathedral was built in the second half of the 14th century and remodelled at the end of the 16th century.

The tomb of King Stephen Batory in St. Mary's Chapel. Its architect was Santi Gucci and the initiator was Queen Anne Jagiellon, wife of the late king.

290 The Cathedral

The late-Gothic Holy Trinity Chapel erected in the 15th century, founded by Queen Sophie, Ladislaus Jagiełło's last wife.

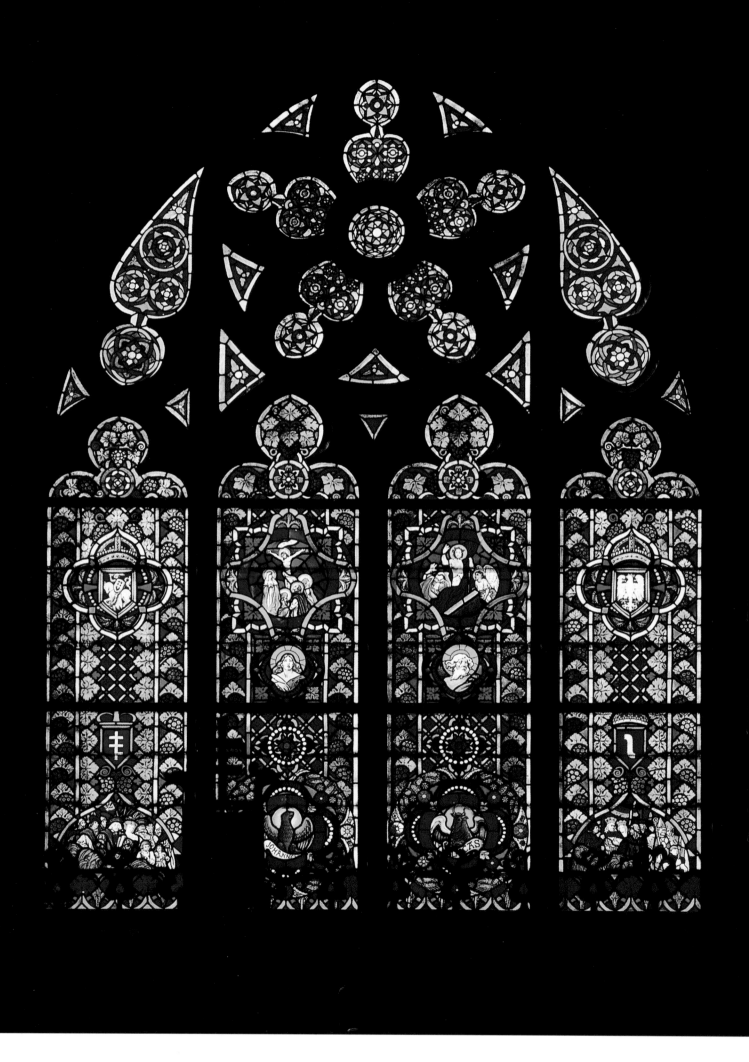

Stained-glass, designed by Włodzimierz Tetmajer, placed in the Gothic window
frames in Queen Sophie's Chapel.

The sarcophagus of Casimir the Great and the memorials dedicated to John III Sobieski and Maria Casimira and Michael Korybut Wiśniowiecki and Eleanor.

294 The Cathedral The stately „Sigismund" Bell cast by Jan Behem of Nuremberg in 1520. It weighs 10 980 kg.

Gen. Władysław Sikorski's funeral. He died in the aeroplane crash over Gibraltar in 1943. His mortal remains were entombed in Wawel vaults on 17th September 1993.

One of the stone sculptures of saints on the southern wall of the Vasa Chapel.

Christmas decorations on Wawel Hill.

The small domes of the Sigismund Tower and the Clock Tower.

The Clock Tower and the Tower of the Silver Bells, also called the Curates' Tower.

300 The Cathedral

A panorama of Cracow with Wawel Castle as seen from St. Stanislaus Kostka's Church in the district of Dębniki, on the other side of the Vistula.

302 The Cathedral   A view of the city and the environs as seen from the top of Marshal Józef Piłsudski's Mound.

Copyright © „Biały Kruk" Publishing House, Ltd.
Ul. Kapelanka 1a/1
30-347 Krakow, Poland
Phone/fax: 00 48/12 267 23 33
Mobile: 00 48/601 714 293
First edition
ISBN 83-907760-5-7